1939~45 PORTFOLIO
AMERICAN ARMOUR

1939~45 PORTFOLIO

AMERICAN ARMOUR

Simon Forty

First published 1981

ISBN 0 7110 1052 8

Design by Robert C. Wilcockson

Published by Ian Allan Ltd, Shepperton, Surrey,
and printed by Ian Allan Printing Ltd at their
works at Coombelands in Runnymede, England

Acknowledgement
All the photographs in this book were obtained from the
IMPERIAL WAR MUSEUM
We believe this book reflects the wealth of material held
by the Museum and which is available to view by the
general public. We must express our thanks to the staff
of the Photographic Library for their considerable help.

INTRODUCTION

In December 1941 America entered World War 2 and she did so almost completely unprepared to fight a major land-based campaign. The US Army had but two armoured divisions, each with about 150 tanks — mostly light — and American industry was building armoured fighting vehicles that were little match for their German counterparts. It would not be until the Operation Torch landings in North Africa in 1942 that America would be able to take the offensive, and when this happened her armies were badly mauled at Kasserine by the Germans. Yet, by 1945, the American tank industry had built over 88,000 tanks — almost four times the number built by Germany 1939-45 (c24,000) — and her armoured vehicles had fought for almost every Allied power in every major war theatre, a considerable achievement by both the industrial manufacturers and designers and the Ordnance Department.

The blitzkrieg tactics of the Germans in the early stages of the war had had a profound effect on American doctrines on the use and design of armoured vehicles. The most immediate on the tank industry was the cancellation of the M2A1 medium tank project which was to have provided the American Army with its main fighting vehicle — a 37mm-armed infantry tank that would have stood little chance against the German Pzkpfw III and IV, the latter armed with a 75mm main gun. The tank that took the place of the M2A1 medium was the M3 — later to be called the Lee/Grant by the British — very much a stopgap design that combined with the existing M2A1 hull layout an unwieldy, sponson-mounted 75mm main gun with limited traverse. While the M3 medium series performed valiantly in the field it was never more than an interim measure until a better-designed project — the M4 medium — could be planned and produced.

The pilot M4 was built in February 1941 and in October 1942 the first production M4s saw action for the first time with the British forces at El Alamein. Over 44,000 Shermans (as the British called the M4) of all marks and variants were built 1942-46 and it was the single most important vehicle for Allied armoured formations while it was in production. Durable, easily mass-produced, the M4 highlighted American armour doctrines at the time, being mechanically reliable and very dependable but, by the time of the opening of the European front in 1944, outgunned and underarmoured when fighting the later German vehicles armed with the 88mm main gun. It was produced in vast numbers because the American Army felt that it needed quantities of vehicles, even if they were outclassed by the opposition, rather than stopping the production lines to produce smaller numbers of more powerful heavy tanks. It would be only after the Ardennes offensive of winter 1944/45 during which the German armour savaged its American opposition that the Ordnance Department was able to force the Army Ground Forces (AGF) to accept shipments of the T26E3 (later to be standardised as the M26 Pershing) to Europe.

The vehicles upon which the AGF had placed their hopes of destroying the heavily armoured German tanks were the series of tank destroyers — the M10 (armed with a 3in gun), the M36 (90mm) and the M18 (76mm). These were lightly armoured, extremely fast, open turreted vehicles which were supposed to use hit and run tactics to destroy their slower but better armoured rivals. There are three basic parameters in the building of an armoured fighting vehicle — armour protection, battlefield mobility and firepower — and a preponderance of any one of these leads directly to a reduction of the others. The tank destroyers sacrificed protection — having extremely thin armour on the sides and an open topped turret — for battlefield mobility, while their firepower was certainly as good if not better than the German tanks.

This idea of splitting armour into two schools — the basic armour and the tank destroyers — was based on proposals put forward after the lessons of 1940 had been assimilated. During the 1930s the American tank formations and designs had been under the control of the infantry, but on 10 July 1940 the pendulum swung too far the other way with the creation of the Armored Force under Brig Adna Chaffee, a formation based on the almost 'private army' type of doctrine which felt that armour should be employed in special corps — all conquering armoured forces to be used by themselves. Opposition to this 'armour above all' approach was headed by the commanding general of the AGF, Lesley McNair, who felt that a more integrated infantry/armour team was necessary. This more balanced view led to the redesignation of the Armored Force in 1943 when it became the Armored Command. At the same time the Tank Destroyer Center in Fort Hood, Texas, was set up to continue the building up of this force, placing the onus of destroying enemy armoured vehicles on the tank destroyers and thereby, it was hoped, enabling conventional armoured forces to pursue their integrated infantry tasks without the temptation of entering 'private duels' with enemy tanks. At the end of the war the tank destroyer arm was disbanded as it had been found that the idea of a fast, mobile reserve of upgunned vehicles to seek out and destroy enemy armoured thrusts was not as effective an anti-tank deterrent as a better armoured and better gunned conventional tank — which has led to the main battle tank concepts of today. However, it must be said that the Americans, with the need to transport their armoured vehicles over vast distances to the battle front and fighting an offensive war which entailed crossing natural obstacles over hastily built and improvised bridges, were certainly justified in their apprehensions about heavy tanks.

In 1943 the Armored Force became the Armored Command and all armoured units were integrated into the AGF, with all units assigned to corps and armies — including those non-divisional formations that had not been attached to the 16 armoured divisions raised by the American Army. The basic armoured formation, therefore, was the division, which saw armour and motorised infantry set up in an integrated formation. The armoured division organisation underwent a number of changes during World War 2, of which two were particularly important (see tables). The first major change, effective 1 March 1942, resulted in the 'heavy' division and the next major alteration, effective 15 September 1943, produced the 'light' division. The former altered the old armoured brigade formation, creating two combat commands (CCs) and two armoured regiments, with three battalions in each regiment — two medium and one light. The CCs gave more flexibility and their composition could be altered to fit the battle situation. The 1943 reorganisation reduced the tank strength by replacing the six tank battalions in two regiments with three tank battalions, thus reducing the overall divisional strength by nearly 4,000. The reorganisation took time to implement and some units (1st Armored, for example) did not change until well into 1944. Both these major reorganisations and the other minor ones were mainly to increase the infantry element, slimming down support formations and increasing medium tank strength at the expense of the light, thereby producing a much more modern unit, forerunner of the present day 'square' brigades.

By late 1943/early 1944, therefore, American armoured formations and American armour had been reorganised and redesigned and production was in full swing. The major beneficiaries of this production, outside the American Army, were the British, for whom, through the Lend-Lease agreements, much of the armour was destined. Indeed, between the Matilda, which was called the 'Queen of the battlefield' on its arrival in North Africa, and the Centurion which was one of the most successful of postwar AFVs, the British had nothing to compare with the American vehicles. British use of American armour began in 1941 with the M3 light tank which they nicknamed the Honey, and they also received a few of the M5 Stuart, a design based on the M3 chassis, in 1943-44. However, after the M3 light, the most important addition to the British arsenal in the desert was the M3 medium, produced in two forms called the Lee and the Grant. This vehicle, as has already been described, was very much a stopgap while the M4 medium was produced, but it played an effective and important part in the desert battles, over 600 arriving before October 1942 when the first M4 mediums came, just in time for the battle of El Alamein. After the arrival of the M4 Sherman, the M3s were shipped to Burma where they performed with great efficiency. Also available for El Alamein were 90 M7 howitzer motor carriages, armed with a 105mm howitzer, which the British called the Priest. When these vehicles began to equip the field artillery battalions of American armoured divisions the British received Canadian-built versions of the M7, called the Sexton.

The main American tank received by the British, however, was the M4 medium, the Sherman, of which over 40,000 of all types were built. More than 1,600 (mainly in the M4A4 version) had been delivered to the British by 1943, and that total increased throughout the war. The British made considerable modifications to their Shermans, including a whole range of 'funnies' — flame throwers, mine clearers, etc — and the upgunning of the vehicle with the British 17pdr gun, which produced possibly the best armed version of the Sherman — the Sherman Firefly. This modification had already been made effectively on the M10, of which the British had received a number, to produce the Achilles.

In this book there are examples of American armour being used by many nationalities showing the wide range of users and vehicles in Europe during 1943-45, giving a good representation of the effect of American armour on the European fronts. Also included are some vehicles which while not being 'armour' as such, are either related to the armoured vehicles in the book or were part of the American armoured divisions — the M2/M3 halftracks for example. All the photographs, unless specifically noted, are from the Imperial War Museum, Lambeth, and I would like to thank all the members of the Photographic Library for their assistance in the research for this book. The superb line drawings are by Kenneth M. Jones who has also assisted with the technical information in the captions as has Simon Dunstan.

Finally, the main sources for the information both in the captions and data sections are the following publications: P. Chamberlain and C. Ellis' *British and American Tanks of World War II* (Arms and Armour Press, 1969) which is the best book on the subject; *US Army Handbook, Patton's Third Army at War, Fifth Army at War* (all G. Forty, Ian Allan Ltd) and C. Foss's *Armoured Fighting Vehicles of the World* (Ian Allan Ltd, 1977) which provides more on World War II vehicles than might be expected.

A Comparison of the Organisations of the Armoured Division 1942/43

Table 1: Armoured Division, T/O 17 of 1 March 1942

Entire Div	14,620
Div HQ	307
HQ Coy	111
Service Coy	160
Armd Sig Coy	256
Armd Recce Bn	872
Armd Regts (2)	2,424
Armd Field Arty Bns (3)	709
Armd Inf Regt	2,389
Armd Engr Bn	1,174
Div Trains	1,948
Attached Medical	414
Attached Chaplain	14

Principal Armament

Rifles .30cal	1,628
Carbines .30cal	6,042
Pistols .45cal	3,850
LMGs .30cal	237
LMGs (ground) .30cal	54
MGs HB .50cal	103
SMGs (inc on ord vehicles)	1,654
SMGs (on ¼ ton trucks)	506
Mortars 60mm	57
Mortars 81mm	27
ATk Guns SP	126
ATk Guns Towed	68
Hows 105mm SP	54
Assault Guns SP	42
Lt Tanks (w/armament)	158
Med Tanks (w/armament)	232
Armd Cars Recce (w/armament)	79
M2 Halftracks (w/armament)	691
M3 Halftracks (w/o/armament)	42
Scout Car (w/armament)	40
Other Vehicles (inc trailers)	2,146

Table 2: Armoured Division, T/O 17 of 15 September 1943

Entire Div	10,937
Div HQ	164
Tank Bns (3)	729
Inf Bns (3)	1,001
CC HQ & HQ Coy (2)	184
Div Trains HQ & HQ Coy	103
CCR HQ	8
Field Arty	1,623
Auxiliary Units:	
Cav Recce Sqn (Mechanised)	935
Engr Bn	693
Med Bn	417
Ord Bn	762
Sig Coy	302
MP Pl	91
Div HQ Coy	138
Band	58
Attached Medical	261
Attached Chaplain	8

Principal Armament

Rifles .30cal	2,063
Carbines .30cal	5,286
MGs .30cal	465
MGs .50cal	404
Mortars 60mm	63
Mortars 81mm	30
ATk Rocket Launchers	607
Hows 57mm	30
Hows 75mm	17
Hows 105mm	54
Med Tanks	186
Lt Tanks	77
Armd Cars	54
Halftracks carriers	455
Halftracks 81mm Mortar Carriers	18
Vehicles All Types (except boats & a/c)	2,650
Less Combat Types	1,761

Armoured Division

(Source: T/O17 and allied tables from 15 September 1943)

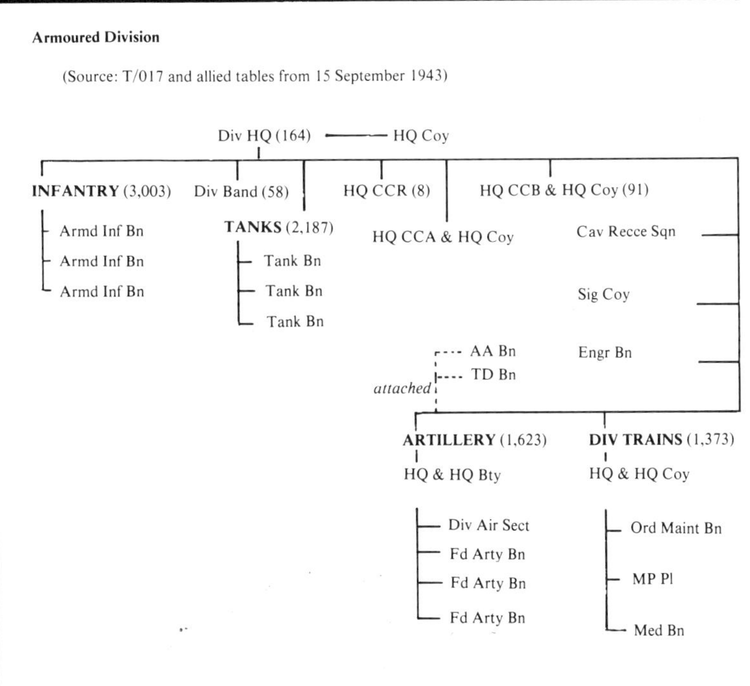

Examples of Distributions of vehicles in the US Armoured Division of 15 September 1943

Armoured Infantry Battalion

Bn HQ $4\times\frac{1}{4}$ ton trucks, $2\times$M3 halftracks.
HQ Coy: *Coy HQ:* HQ Sect $1\times\frac{1}{4}$ ton truck, $1\times$M3 halftrack; AM&S Sect $1\times2\frac{1}{2}$ ton truck, 1×1 ton trailer; Maint Sect $1\times\frac{1}{4}$ ton truck, $1\times$M3 halftrack, 1×1 ton trailer. *Bn Recce Pl* $5\times\frac{1}{4}$ ton trucks, $1\times$M3 halftrack. *Mortar Pl* $1\times$M3 halftrack, $3\times$M21 81mm mortar carriers. *MG Pl* $3\times$M3 halftracks. *Assault Gun Pl* $2\times$M3 halftracks, $3\times$M7 105mm hows, $4\times$M10 ammo trailers.
Rifle Coy: *Coy HQ:* HQ Sect $1\times\frac{1}{4}$ ton truck, $1\times$M3 halftrack; AM&S Sect $2\times2\frac{1}{2}$ ton trucks, 2×1 ton trailers; Maint Sect $1\times\frac{1}{4}$ ton truck, $1\times$M3 halftrack, 1×1 ton trailer. *ATk Pl* $1\times\frac{1}{4}$ ton truck, $3\times$M3 halftracks, $3\times$57mm guns. Three *Rifle Pls* of five squads — three rifle, one mortar and one LMG: each squad $1\times$M3 halftrack.
Service Coy: *Coy HQ:* HQ Sect $1\times\frac{3}{4}$ ton comd car; AM&S Sect $1\times2\frac{1}{2}$ ton truck, 1×1 ton trailer; Maint Sect $1\times\frac{1}{4}$ ton truck, $1\times2\frac{1}{2}$ ton truck, 1×1 ton trailer; Bn Admin & Personnel Sect $1\times2\frac{1}{2}$ ton truck, 1×1 ton trailer. *Bn Supply & Tptn Pl* $1\times\frac{1}{4}$ ton truck, $1\times\frac{3}{4}$ ton truck, $9\times2\frac{1}{2}$ ton trucks, 5×1 ton trailers, $4\times$M10 ammo trailers. *Bn Maint Pl* $1\times\frac{1}{4}$ ton truck, $1\times$M3 halftrack, $2\times2\frac{1}{2}$ ton trucks, 1×6 ton heavy wrecker, $1\times$M32 ARV, 2×1 ton trailers.

Armoured Field Artillery Battalion

Bn HQ $4\times\frac{1}{4}$ ton trucks, $1\times$M3 halftrack.
HQ Bty: *Bty HQ:* HQ Sect $1\times\frac{1}{4}$ ton truck; AM&S Sect $1\times2\frac{1}{2}$ ton truck, 1×1 ton trailer; Maint Sect $1\times\frac{1}{4}$ ton truck, $1\times$M3 halftrack, 1×1 ton trailer; Obs, Recce & Liaison Pl: Liaison Sect $1\times$M3 halftrack; Recce Sect $1\times\frac{1}{4}$ ton truck, $1\times$M3 halftrack, Forward Obs Sect: $3\times$M4 tanks. *Ops Pl:* Op & Fire Direction Sect $3\times$M3 halftracks; Comm Sect $2\times\frac{3}{4}$ ton trucks, $1\times$M3 halftrack; Exec Sect $1\times\frac{1}{4}$ ton truck, $1\times\frac{1}{4}$ ton trailer, $1\times\frac{3}{4}$ ton truck, $1\times$M3 halftrack, $2\times$L5 lt planes.
Field Arty Bty: *Bty HQ:* HQ Sect $1\times\frac{1}{4}$ ton truck, $1\times$M3 halftrack; AM&S Sect $1\times2\frac{1}{2}$ ton truck, 1×1 ton trailer; Maint Sect $1\times\frac{1}{4}$ ton truck, $1\times$M3 halftrack, 1×1 ton trailer. *Firing Bty:* Recce Sect $1\times\frac{1}{4}$ ton truck, $1\times$M3 halftrack; Ammo Sect $2\times$M3 halftracks, $2\times$M10 ammo trailers; Fire Control Sect $2\times$M3 halftracks; Six Howitzer Sects each of $1\times$M7 105mm SP how, $1\times$M10 ammo trailer.
Service Bty: *Bty HQ:* HQ Sect $1\times\frac{3}{4}$ ton truck; AM&S Sect $1\times2\frac{1}{2}$ ton truck, 1×1 ton trailer; Maint Sect $1\times\frac{1}{4}$ ton truck, $1\times2\frac{1}{2}$ ton truck, 1×1 ton trailer; Bn Admin & Personnel Sect $1\times2\frac{1}{2}$ ton truck, 1×1 ton trailer. *Bn Maint Pl* $1\times\frac{1}{4}$ ton truck, $2\times2\frac{1}{2}$ ton trucks, 2×1 ton trailers, 1×6 ton heavy wrecker, $2\times$M32 ARV. *Bn Supply & Tptn Pl* $1\times\frac{1}{4}$ ton truck, $2\times\frac{3}{4}$ ton trucks, $16\times2\frac{1}{2}$ ton trucks, 7×1 ton trailers, $9\times$M10 ammo trailers.

Cavalry Recce Squadron

HQ & HQ Service Tp: *Sqn HQ:* HQ Sect $2\times\frac{1}{4}$ ton trucks, $2\times$M3 halftracks; Comm Sect $4\times\frac{1}{4}$ ton trucks, $3\times$M8 armd cars, $1\times$M3 halftrack; Sqn Admin & Personnel Sect $1\times\frac{1}{4}$ ton truck, $1\times2\frac{1}{2}$ ton truck, 1×1 ton trailer.
HQ Service Tp: *TP HQ:* HQ Sect $1\times\frac{1}{4}$ ton truck; AM&S Sect $1\times2\frac{1}{2}$ ton truck, 1×1 ton trailer; maint Sect $1\times$M3 halftrack, 1×1 ton trailer; Tptn Sect $1\times\frac{1}{4}$ ton truck, $6\times2\frac{1}{2}$ ton trucks, 4×1 ton trailers, $2\times$M10 ammo trailers. *Sqn Maint Pl* $1\times\frac{1}{4}$ ton truck, $1\times$M8 armd car, $1\times$M32 ARV, $1\times$M3 halftrack, 1×6 ton heavy wrecker, $2\times2\frac{1}{2}$ ton trucks, 2×1 ton trailers. *Sqn Supply Sect* $3\times2\frac{1}{2}$ ton trucks, 3×1 ton trailers.
Recce Tps: *Tp HQ:* HQ Sect $3\times\frac{1}{4}$ ton trucks, $2\times$M8 armd cars; AM&S Sect $3\times$M3 halftracks, $1\times2\frac{1}{2}$ ton truck, 4×1 ton trailers; Maint Sect $1\times\frac{1}{4}$ ton truck, $1\times$M8 armd car, $1\times$M3 halftrack, 1×1 ton trailer. Three *Recce Pls* each of: Armd Car Sect $3\times$M8 armd cars; Scout Sect $6\times\frac{1}{4}$ ton trucks.
Assault Gun Tp: *Tp HQ:* HQ Sect $1\times\frac{1}{4}$ ton truck, $1\times$M3 halftrack; AM&S Sect $1\times2\frac{1}{2}$ ton truck, 1×1 ton trailer; Maint Sect $1\times\frac{1}{4}$ ton truck, $1\times$M3 halftrack, $1\times$lt ARV. Four *Assault Gun Pls of:* Pl HQ $1\times$M3 halftrack; Ammo Sect $1\times$M3 halftrack, $1\times$M10 ammo trailer; Gun Sect $2\times$M8 75mm carriage hows, $2\times$M10 ammo trailers.
Lt Tank Coy: *Coy HQ:* HQ Sect $1\times\frac{1}{4}$ ton truck, $2\times$M5 lt tanks; AM&S Sect $1\times2\frac{1}{2}$ ton truck, 1×1 ton trailer; Maint Sect $1\times\frac{1}{4}$ ton truck, $1\times$M3 halftrack, $1\times$lt ARV. Three *Lt Tank Pls* of: $5\times$M5 lt tanks.

Tank Battalion

Bn HQ: HQ Sect $4\times\frac{1}{4}$ ton trucks, $2\times$M3 halftracks; Tank Sect $2\times$M4 tanks.
HQ Coy: *Coy HQ:* HQ Sect $1\times\frac{1}{4}$ ton truck, $1\times$M3 halftrack; AM&S Sect $1\times2\frac{1}{2}$ ton truck, 1×1 ton trailer; Maint Sect $1\times\frac{1}{4}$ ton truck, $1\times$M3 halftrack. *Bn Recce Pl* $5\times\frac{1}{4}$ ton trucks, $1\times$M3 halftrack. *Mortar Pl* $1\times$M3 halftrack, $3\times$M21 81mm mortar carriers. *Assault Gun Pl* $2\times$M3 halftracks, $3\times$M4 tanks (105mm hows), $4\times$M10 ammo carriers.
Med Tank Coy: *Coy HQ:* HQ Sect $1\times\frac{1}{4}$ ton truck, $2\times$M4 tanks, $1\times$M4 (105mm how); AM&S Sect $1\times2\frac{1}{2}$ ton truck, 1×1 ton trailer; Maint Sect $1\times\frac{1}{4}$ ton truck, $1\times$M3 halftrack, $1\times$M32 ARV. Three *Tank Pls* each of $5\times$M4 med tanks.

Lt Tank Coy: Coy HQ: HQ Sect $1 \times \frac{1}{4}$ ton truck, $2 \times$M5 lt tanks; AM&S Sect $1 \times 2\frac{1}{2}$ ton truck, 1×1 ton trailer; Maint Sect $1 \times \frac{1}{4}$ ton truck, $1 \times$M3 halftrack, $1 \times$lt ARV. Three *Tank Pls* each of $5 \times$M5 lt tanks.

Service Coy: Coy HQ: HQ Sect $1 \times \frac{1}{4}$ ton truck; AM&S Sect $1 \times 2\frac{1}{2}$ ton truck, 1×1 ton trailer; Maint Sect $1 \times \frac{1}{4}$ ton truck, $1 \times 2\frac{1}{2}$ ton truck, 1×1 ton trailer; Bn Admin & Personnel Sect $1 \times 2\frac{1}{2}$ ton truck, 1×1 ton trailer. *Bn Maint Pl* $1 \times \frac{1}{4}$ ton truck, $1 \times \frac{3}{4}$ ton truck, $2 \times 2\frac{1}{2}$ ton trucks, 2×1 ton trailer, $2 \times$M32 ARV, $2 \times$heavy wreckers. *Bn Supply & Tptn Pl* $1 \times \frac{1}{4}$ ton truck, $1 \times \frac{3}{4}$ ton truck, $29 \times 2\frac{1}{2}$ ton trucks, 15×1 ton trailers, $13 \times$M10 ammo trailers.

The American Armoured Divisions of World War II

Division	Nickname	Battle Honours
1st	Old Ironsides	North Africa, (Tunisia), and Italy
2nd	Hell on wheels	North Africa (Algeria and French Morocco)
3rd	Spearhead	North West Europe, Normandy, Northern France, Rhineland, Ardennes-Alsace, Central Europe
4th	None (Occasionally called 'Breakthrough)	As for 3rd
5th	Victory	As for 3rd
6th	Super Sixth	As for 3rd
7th	Lucky Seventh	As for 3rd
8th	Iron Snake, Thundering Herd, Tornado	As for 3rd less Normandy
9th	Phantom	As for 8th
10th	Tiger	As for 8th
11th	Thunderbolt	As for 8th less Northern France
12th	Hellcat	As for 11th
13th	Black Cat	As for 11th
14th	Liberator	As for 11th
16th	None	Rhineland, Central Europe
20th	None	As for 16th

The Armoured divisions' shoulder insignia consisted of a triangle divided into three with the top yellow, the bottom left blue and the bottom right red. The division number was in black in the yellow section. In the centre was an armoured vehicle track in black under a red lightning bolt.

Organic Components of the Activated Armoured Division of World War II

Div	Armd Inf Bns			Tk Bns			Div Arty	Armd Arty	Fd Bns	Cav Recce Sqn	Armd Eng Bn	Armd Med Bn	Armd Ord Bn	Armd Sig Coy
1	6	11	14	1	4	13	27	68	91	81	16	47	123	141
2	41*	63*	67*	–	–	–	14	78	92	82	17	48	2	142
3	32*	33*	36*	–	–	–	54	67	391	83	23	45	3	143
4	10	51	53	8	35	37	22	66	94	25	24	4	126	144
5	15	46	47	10	34	81	47	71	95	85	22	75	127	145
6	9	44	50	15	68	69	128	212	231	86	25	76	128	146
7	23	38	48	17	31	40	434	440	489	87	33	77	129	147
8	7	49	58	18	36	80	398	399	405	88	53	78	130	148
9	27	52	60	2	14	19	3	16	73	89	9	2	131	149
10	20	54	61	3	11	21	419	420	423	90	55	80	132	150
11	21	55	63	22	41	42	490	491	492	41	56	81	133	151
12	17	56	66	23	43	714	493	494	495	92	119	82	134	152
13	16	59	67	24	45	46	496	497	498	93	124	83	135	153
14	19	62	68	25	47	43	499	500	501	94	125	84	136	154
16	18	64	69	5	16	26	393	396	397	23	216	216	137	156
20	8	65	70	9	20	27	412	413	414	30	220	220	138	160

*These units were armoured regiments during World War II.

Above left: British Stuart Is: note lack of sponson machine guns, riveted hull, welded turret and cupola.

Above: M3A3 with redesigned, all-welded hull and increased stowage. This vehicle has a .30cal machine gun on a pintle mount, sand shields and a spotlight on the turret top.

Left: British M3A1 Stuart moving towards Caen, 1944. The star and circle marking on the turret, although an American national marking, was used by many Allied vehicles after D-Day. On the sponson housings, at the front, circular armour patches show clearly where the twin machine guns of earlier M3 models have been removed. Fired in tandem by the driver, these machine guns were discarded to provide extra stowage space and to reduce weight. Note also the German jerricans on the right of the photograph next to the overturned cart.

Above: **M5A1** passing through a French town in the Lorient area. This photograph shows one of the main changes to the basic M5 which led to the M5A1, the increased turret extension for radio installation. On the side of the turret is a pintle mount for a .30cal machine gun and the hull side national marking has been painted over to reduce points of reference for enemy anti-tank gunners.

Left: **M5A1** equipped with Cullin hedgerow device cuts its way through a thicket in Normandy. Just below the covered .30cal machine gun can be seen the detachable armoured fairing which was provided to protect the AA mount on later versions of the tank.

Above right: **M5** advancing towards St Lo, July 1944. The jeep on the left has an anti-wire device on the front, an interesting field modification stemming from the enemy stretching wire at head height across roads — particularly dangerous to motorcyclists and jeeps.

Right: **M5** crashing through an improvised roadblock at the entrance to Harze, Belgium. This photograph gives a good view of the .30cal AA machine gun and its magazine box. The M1919A1 .30cal Browning machine gun had a rate of fire of 450-600 rounds per minute from a disintegrating link belt.

Right: The M5A1 Stuart in British service, with whom it was designated the Stuart VI. A number of M5s and M5A1s were delivered to the British in 1943-44 and saw action in NW Europe.

Below: Men of the light tank platoon of US 5th Infantry Division read their mail beside their M5A1 outside Schwanheim, Germany, March 1945. Note the .30cal ammunition box on the right and the 'MENU 5' ration box on the left. Field ration B, known as 10 in 1 (which can be read on the box) was the standard field ration of the US Army, containing enough food for 10 men for one day — one cold and two hot meals each. The crew themselves display a variety of personal uniforms, with the man at far right wearing one of the much-coveted tank windcheaters.

Right: An **M5** charges up a river bank near Demfront, France, 1944. The photograph shows the firepower of the M5 light tank — three .30cal machine guns (AA, bow and coax) and one 37mm M6 main gun. The M6 37mm main gun was little use against German armoured vehicles. With a muzzle velocity of 2,545ft/sec it could penetrate 48mm of armour at 500yd, but it did give the M5 a useful armament against soft-skinned vehicles and infantry targets.

Below: **M5** of the US Third Army covers infantrymen as they recover their previously abandoned jeep, somewhere in Luxembourg during the Ardennes campaign, winter 1944/45. The jeep has an improvised wire cutter fixed to the front.

Left: M5A1 passing a knocked out German PzKpfw V Panther whose main 75mm KwK42 L/70 gun has been blown off at the mantlet.

Below: American armour passing a British infantry Bren carrier (with a roll of barbed wire on the back) outside Rome. The American column is headed by an M5 (note British type bridging circle on nose which indicated to engineers the bridging weight); behind are M8 armoured cars.

Right: M5A1s and an M4 rolling towards Germany, 16 November 1944. The M5A1 in the centre is fitted with a Cullin hedgerow device; this was a field modification from the beach defences in Normandy and was particularly effective in the bocage country.

Below right: In February 1944, Fifth Army attacked the Italian coastal towns of Nettuno and Anzio in a full amphibious attack, during which US VI Corps bore the brunt of the fighting. These M5s are equipped for wading and are being landed at Nettuno from a landing ship tank (LST). They are probably part of the reinforcements which landed in April after the bridgehead was secure; these consisted of US 45th Infantry Division and if these vehicles belong to that unit they would be elements of 45th Recon Troop.

Above right: Howitzer motor carriage (HMC) M8 — a 75mm howitzer in an open-topped turret mounted on an M5 chassis. This photograph shows clearly the modified hatches for driver and co-driver on the hull front necessitated by the larger turret.

Centre right: HMC M8 advancing towards Marigny, west of St Lo, 25 July 1944, during the breakout from the Normandy landings. The area had seen heavy bombardment and knocked out vehicles can be seen on both sides of the road — to the left a jeep and trailer, to the right a Sherman, which, from the damage to its undersides, seems to have received a direct hit which has exploded stowed ammunition. The M4 could carry up to 97 rounds of ammunition for its 75mm main gun and 4,750 rounds of .30cal ammunition for its secondary armament. Initial types had poor ammunition stowage protection, which accounts for the applique armour on vital points. Later types had 'wet' stowage.

Below, far left: HMC M8 giving fire support. Littered around the vehicle are the containers for 75mm ammunition. Just visible above the turret rim are the heads of the gunners and the periscopic sight, and the photograph also shows typical equipment stowage on turret sides and rear decking.

Right: HMC M8 and M4A1 (76mm) preparing to fire on German positions near Berenton, France, 5 August 1944.

Below: HMC M8s rumble through Montreuil en route to Marigny during the breakout from Normandy, 25 July 1944. The photograph illustrates the length of the .50cal M2HB AA machine gun — 5ft 5in. This Browning machine gun was capable of firing 450-500 rounds per minute from a disintegrating link belt feed which was contained in a box on the left hand side of the gun.

Above: **M24 Chaffees** drive down the Charlottenburg Chaussee during the victory in Europe celebrations held in Berlin. This photograph shows how visible the white Allied star and circle markings were at a distance: a perfect aiming point for enemy anti-tank gunners, which accounts for the often seen painting-out of the marking in the field.

Top right: **M24 Chaffee** at speed in the snow, NW Europe, 1945, showing the AA machine gun mount peculiar to this vehicle. The M24 had a top road speed of 35mph and a top cross-country speed of approximately 25mph.

Right: **M24 Chaffee** in white, winter camouflage. The side skirts are missing from this vehicle and the triangular brackets to which they were attached can be seen. When compared to the M5 Stuart, which it replaced, the M24 was a major advance and, indeed, saw considerable service in the armies of many nations postwar. Immensely agile, the M24 was well armed for a light tank with an M6 75mm main gun.

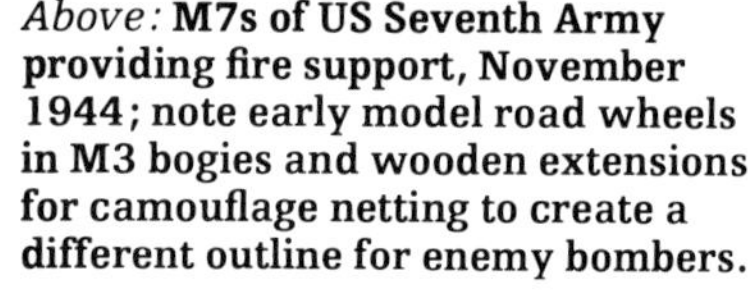

Above: **M7s of US Seventh Army providing fire support, November 1944; note early model road wheels in M3 bogies and wooden extensions for camouflage netting to create a different outline for enemy bombers.**

Left: **M7 of British 3rd Division in action overlooking Caen between Hermanville and Beuville.**

Above right: **HMC M7 advancing north-west from the Marne past French civilians repairing the road. Note .50cal machine gun in pulpit mount, driver's hatch open, M4 bogies and jerricans stowed on the front (W on furthest point left indicates water).**

Right: **HMC M7 of the Free French 2nd Armoured Division 'somewhere in England', where an African soldier is attending to the 105mm howitzer. The unit markings have been deleted by the censor, although the Free French one has been left on the side. This photograph shows the difference between the M7 and M7B1 ammunition protection — the lack of an armoured flap leaves the ammunition very unprotected. This is a late model M7, having M3 bogies but a cast one-piece nose.**

Far left, inset: HMC M7B1 by the Dragon's Teeth of the Siegfried Line, February 1945. The M7B1 differed from the M7 in being based on the M4A3 as opposed to the M3 chassis. It had, therefore, a cast one-piece nose, M4 bogies with trailing return rollers and hinged side plates for added ammunition protection.

Left inset: During the Battle of the Bulge in December 1944, an M7B1 is given fire instructions over a field telephone (note reel of wire to rear of vehicle). On a small table to the right of the photograph, the 105mm two-piece (projectile and charge) ammunition is being removed from its packing containers prior to firing. The vehicle itself has a field-fitted storage rack at the front, an M1 carbine hanging from the side, and just visible above the side plating can be seen a loader with a 105mm projectile.

Left: A US M7 moving past elements of 314th Infantry Regiment, 79th Division (note 79-314-I marking on trailers. Usually the regiment or battalion code was not separated from its branch/service symbol, but in the case of I for Infantry and O for Ordnance, to save confusion with numbers, a dash was inserted between the two). Six of the seven crew can be seen aboard the vehicle, four in the gun area, one in the pulpit mount and the driver, whose hull-front hatch is open.

Above: **The limber vehicle for the M12 was the M30, based on the M3 chassis as well. This US Ninth Army vehicle is crossing the River Roer, February 1945.**

Below: **GMC M12, with an M1918 155mm gun of French World War 1 design on an M3 chassis with M4 bogies (note trailing return rollers). Used in the later years of World War 2 for long-range bombardment, the M12 had a spade at the rear to cater for recoil.**

Right: Although this appears to be an M3 gun tank, it is in fact an M31 tank recovery vehicle both of whose main guns are dummies — only the .50cal is functional. A door handle can be seen on the sponson gun housing. On the nose there are two early type roadwheels and a tow hitch bolted between the transmission housings. The M31 was fitted with a rear-mounted boom and 60,000lb winch.

Below: An M31 tank recovery vehicle pulls an M4 out of trouble. Note applique armour, camouflage nets and stowage on rear decking of the M4.

Below: **M3 Lee medium tank on training exercise Defiance V in Northern Ireland. The star and stripe American national marking seen on the turret was used on armoured vehicles between 1942 and 1943. The other marking on the outside of the sponson gun housing, which can also be seen on the tank at far right, indicates that these tanks belong to E Company, 2nd Battalion, 13th Armored Regiment of the US 1st Armored Division. They are armed with the early M2 75mm main gun which required a counterbalancing weight on the muzzle, necessary to balance the gyrostabiliser. The M3 medium saw extensive service in north Africa and Burma, and was also used in Italy. By 1944, however, it was considered obsolete, and, indeed, with its unwieldy configuration and high silhouette it was little match for the Axis weaponry.**

Three views of M3s in British service in Burma. *Above left:* **Shows clearly the counterweight on M2 75mm gun muzzle.** *Above* **and** *above right:* **M3s equipped with M3 sponson-mounted guns.**

Right: **M31 tank recovery vehicle, based on the M3 medium chassis, recovering an M4. Note dummy sponson-mounted 75mm gun, riveted hull and rearmounted boom.**

Above: **A camouflaged M4 (105mm) of US 6th Armored Division (the 'Super Sixth') moving through a snowy wood near Bastogne. The 105mm howitzer in the M52 mount proved a very effective fire support weapon. This Sherman has extended tracks to facilitate traction in the soft, snowy going, the later 47-degree hull front and a quick coat of whitewash.**

Top right: **M4 Shermans of a Free French unit (2nd Armoured Division) 'somewhere in England' being serviced prior to the Normandy landings. The Free French marking is half obscured by a passing soldier's head. The Sherman in the foreground has a pistol grip smoke discharger and applique armour on the turret.**

Right: **M4 of the 745th Tank Battalion loads up with ammunition — 75mm (of which the M4 could carry 97 rounds) for the M3 main gun which is housed in an M34A1 gun mount, and .30cal for the bow and coaxially-mounted machine guns. The M4 could carry 4,750 rounds of .30cal ammunition. Note the difference in the hull fronts of the two vehicles in this photograph — the three-piece bolted nose on the left and one-piece cast on the right.**

Left: **M4A3 (76mm) HVSS with M1A1C** main gun; mounted in an M62 gun mount its high velocity armoured piercing round (HVAP) had a muzzle velocity of 3,400ft/sec and could penetrate 133mm of armour at 1,000yd — a considerable improvement on the 70mm at 500yd of the M3 75mm gun. The vehicle picture here has been knocked out and abandoned (all crew hatches open) and the bow and AA machine guns have been removed.

Below left: Naturally camouflaged **M4 (76mm)** of US 3rd Armored Division ('Spearhead') with T23 turret and M1A1 main gun passing a knocked out PzKpfw V Panther near Bovigny, Belgium.

Right: An **M4** of 2nd Armored Division ('Hell on Wheels') moves along an icy road to Dochamp; note applique armour on hull side.

Below: Reworked **M4A2** of 2nd Armoured Division (Free French) moving off an LST on to the Normandy beaches. The armament of this vehicle has been covered to stop corrosion and the 75mm main gun is housed in the older, narrower M34 gun mount.

Above left: Awaiting the invasion of Europe, these M4s are seen in store in England. The M4 in the foreground has an M34A1 gun mount while the rest are equipped with the narrower M34. For storage purposes the ventilators are sealed: note wire guards on periscopes and applique armour on turret sides.

Above: Another view of M4s in an American supply depot in England shortly before the invasion of Europe. Here the left hand row is equipped with the M34A1 mount, while the right has the M34. These Shermans are equipped with the standard M3 75mm gyrostabilised main gun which had proved so effective in the desert. The photograph also gives a good view of the applique armour applied in slabs to the driver's and co-driver's hatches of the M4.

Left: Three M4s (105mm) of US Seventh Army providing fire support from flooded fire positions. The debris includes a quantity of shell boxes and containers: the 105mm howitzer which armed both the M7 and M8 howitzer motor carriages used a two-piece shot and charge round which came in special cylindrical cartons discarded after use.

Above: **While engineers begin repair work on a demolished bridge near Fontainebleau, France, an M4 takes the easy way. This vehicle has the wide M3A1 gun mount, Cullin hedgerow device and extensive sandbagging on the nose, the latter one of the many ways tried to protect the Allied armoured vehicles from the effective anti-tank weapons of the enemy.**

Left: **How many men can you get on a tank? — 1 This 76mm-armed M4 has been field fitted with a framework to support heavy sandbagging upon which men of US Ninth Army are sitting. The tank was attached to 79th Infantry Division and the photograph was taken on 10 April 1945 during the fighting around Essen. Note M3 'Grease Gun' carried by soldier at front left.**

Above: This photograph affords a good comparison between standard M4s armed with M3 75mm main guns and the 76mm armed vehicle in the foreground. The M1A1 76mm main gun was considerably longer than the M3 75mm (118.375in to 168in) and required a different turret to accommodate the extra length and a counterweight. Designated the T23, this turret came from the ill-fated T23 medium tank project. These Shermans belong to the 712th Tank Battalion, attached to 90th Infantry Division, and are pictured outside Bavigne, Luxembourg.

Right: An M4A2 (76mm) HVSS in British service, with whom this type was designated the Sherman IIIAY. This vehicle has a flotation screen framework erected which, in conjunction with two drive propellers, could give a speed of up to 4kts in water. This Duplex Drive (DD) equipment evolved in 1941 and was first used on the Valentine. In June 1944 DD Shermans equipped a brigade of 79th Armoured Division and were the first British tanks on the Normandy beaches.

Left: Infantrymen rest behind an M4. The soldier in the foreground is armed with a later pattern Thompson SMG (cocking handle on side). The photograph shows clearly the usefulness of armoured vehicles on the battlefield aside from their weapons; the close cooperation of tank and infantry was essential and mutually supporting — the tank provided a heavy arms platform and armoured protection to the infantry while the infantry, especially in the bocage country of Normandy and during urban fighting, provided the tank with protection from anti-tank teams and portable anti-tank weapons.

Below left: Heavily snow-camouflaged M4 during the Ardennes campaign, 1944/45. Note the white camouflage smocks of the personnel on the turret.

Right: M4 in a tactical fire position with crewmen checking radio antenna. Visible to the right is the perforated barrel housing of the AA .50cal machine gun. This M4 is equipped with extended grousers on the tracks for better traction in soft going.

Below: M4 (76mm) with M1A1 main gun crossing the River Roer by pontoon bridge. This vehicle has been fitted with concrete armour on the nose to try to increase its chances against the heavier gunned German tanks. As can be imagined, such modifications were of doubtful value and certainly affected the speed and range of the vehicle; the custom was, therefore, frowned upon officially.

Right: **This M4** of 6th Armored Division was knocked out by a German bazooka in Mageret, Belgium. It has extended grousers on the tracks and the entry hole of the projectile can be seen amongst the ruins of the tracks.

Below: **M4 (76mm)** with welded storage strips on its T23 turret (a field modification) passing burning buildings in Aschaffenburg, south-east of Frankfurt. The vehicle belongs to US Seventh Army.

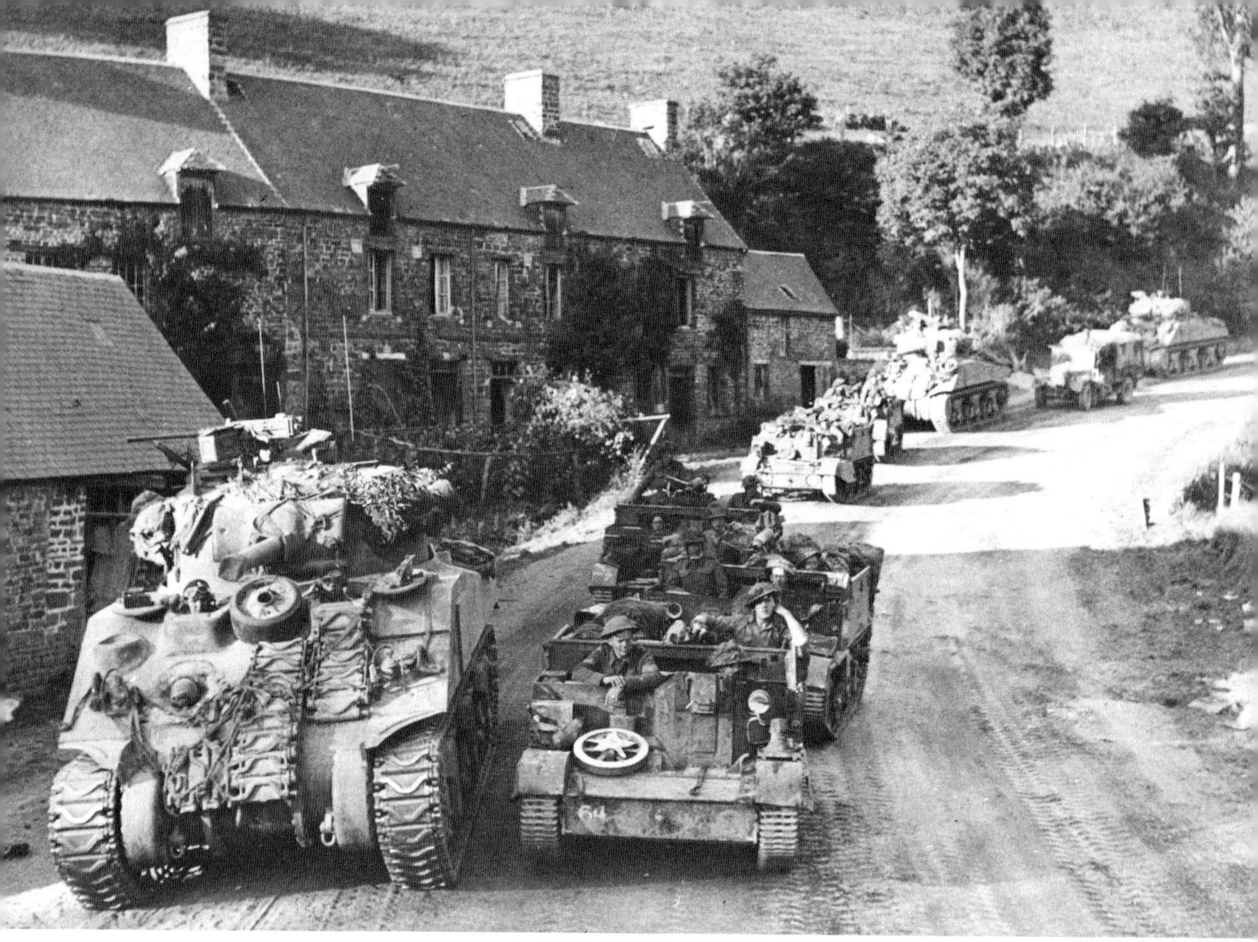

Below: British M4A4 moving at speed through cornfields in the Odon valley.

Above: Another method of increasing protection often seen on M4s was the use of tracks, here on a vehicle from a British unit in Vassy, France. Note three-piece hull, front roadwheel on nose and column of Bren carriers, the second of which has a Vickers .303in machine gun mounted.

Above right: Another common field modification to the front hulls of M4s was the fitting of a stowage rack, apparent here on an M4 making its way through a wooded area; note the enemy's use of felled trees as attempted anti-tank devices.

Right: Another version of the stowage rack can be seen on the foremost of these M4s of US Seventh Army lined up in Volksborg, France. The first three vehicles are M4A1s with the distinctive cast hull.

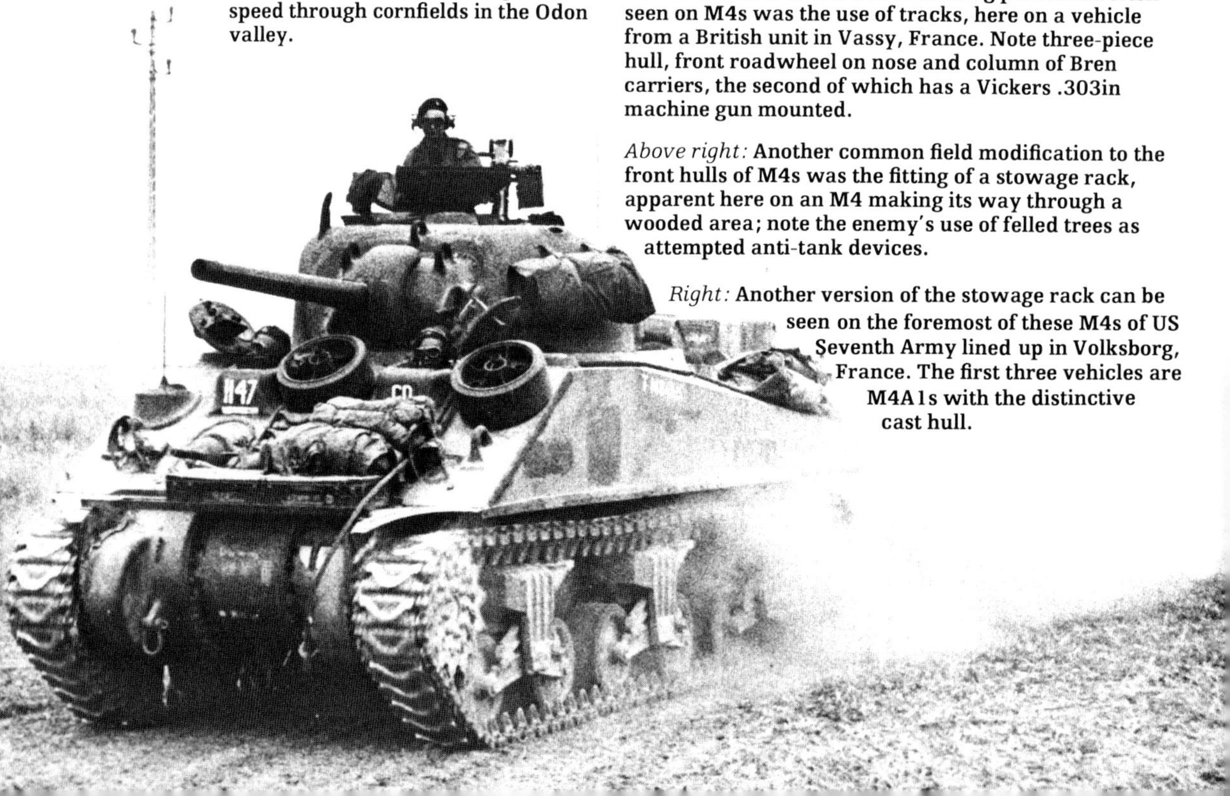

Light Tank M3 Stuart

Crew: 4 (commander, gunner, driver, co-driver)
Length: 14ft 10.75in
16ft 6in (M3A3)
Width: 7ft 4in
8ft 3in (M3A3)
Height: 8ft 3in
7ft 6.5in (M3A1, M3A3)
Weight: 27,400lb (M3)
28,504lb (M3A1)
31,752lb (M3A3)
Armament: 1×37mm M5 or M6 gun (main)
2×.30cal Browning MGs (secondary, hull and coax; plus two in sponsons on M3)
1×.30cal MG (AA)
Armour: 51mm (max)-10mm (min)
Engine: Continental W-670, petrol with seven cylinders developing 250hp or Guiberson T1020 radial diesel with nine cylinders developing 220hp
Max speed: 36mph
20mph approx cross-country
Road range: 70-90 miles

M3A1 (Stuart III) with cast/welded homogenous turret and all-welded hull; note distinctive features of the M3A1 — lack of sponson-mounted machine guns and lack of cupola.

The M3 series was developed from the M2 series in 1940, incorporating lessons learnt from the early campaigns of World War 2. 5,811 were built, of which 500 had the Guiberson diesel engine. By August 1941 an improved version was brought out, the M3A1 with a gyrostabiliser for the gun, power traverse for turret and omission of the two sponson-mounted MGs the M3 had been armed with. The height was reduced by removal of the cupola. 4,621 were built, 211 with diesels. Next version was the M3A2, the first of the series to be all welded instead of riveted: in practice the designation was not used and both types were called M3A1s. Final, and considerably improved, version was the M3A3 which entered production in 1943. 3,427 of these were built and they had a redesigned hull with much increased internal stowage and sandshields. Declared obsolete by late 1943, the M3 remained in use up to the end of the war as an effective reconnaissance tank. One of the first vehicles to be put into service with the British under the Lend-Lease agreements, the M3 series, nicknamed by the British the 'Honey', saw very important service in the desert c1941-2.

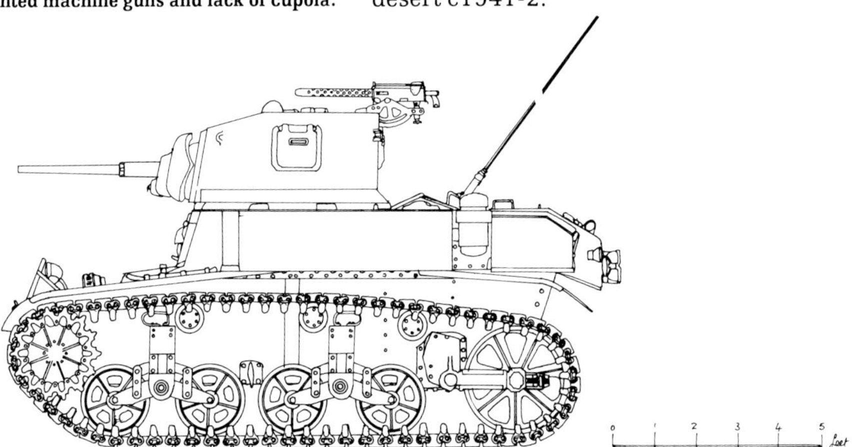

Light Tank M5 Stuart

Crew: 4 (commander, gunner, driver, co-driver)
Length: 14ft 2.75in
15ft 10.5in (M5A1)
Width: 7ft 4.25in
7ft 4.5in (M5A1)
Height: 7ft 6.5in
7ft 10.5in (M5A1)
Weight: 33,000lb
33,950lb (M5A1, loaded)
Armament: 1×37mm M6 gun (main)
2×.30cal Browning MGs (secondary, hull and coax)
1×.30cal Browning MG (AA)

Armour: 67mm (max)-12mm (min)
Engine: Cadillac Twin V8, 220hp
Max speed: 36mph
24mph approx cross-country
Road range: 100 miles

The M5 was a conversion of the earlier M3 Light Tank with a Cadillac transmission and engines. In September 1942 the M5A1 was standardised to bring the M5 up to M3A3 standard. This version, the M5A3, began production in early 1943. The differences included a new turret with added room at the back for radio installations; modifications to the gun mount, vision devices, access hatches and commander's cupola. A later addition was a detachable armour shield to protect the pintle-mounted .50cal MG.

Howitzer Motor Carriage M8

Crew: 4
Length: 16ft 3.5in
Width: 7ft 7in
Height: 7ft 6.5in
Weight: 34,000lb
Armament: 1×75mm howitzer (main)
1×.50cal Browning MG (AA)
Armour: 54mm (max)-10mm (min)
Engine: Cadillac Twin V8, 220hp
Max speed: 36mph
24mph approx cross-country
Road range: 100 miles

The M8 was, basically, an M5 with a different turret to house a 75mm howitzer and, because of the size of this turret, it had alterations to the hull — the drivers' hatches were moved to the hull front. Produced by Cadillac, 1,778 were built and it was only in 1944 that it was replaced as the standard HQ company support weapon in medium tank battalions, by the M4 (105mm) Sherman.

Light Tank M24 Chaffee

Crew: 5 (commander, gunner, loader, driver, co-driver/radio operator)
Length: 18ft (with gun)
16ft 6in (without)
Width: 9ft 8in
Height: 8ft 1.5in
Weight: 36,250lb (empty)
40,500lb (loaded)
Armament: 1×75mm M6 gun (main)
2×.30cal Browning MGs (secondary, hull and coax)
1×.50cal Browning MG (AA)
Armour: 38mm (max)-10mm (min)
Engine: Cadillac twin 44T24 petrol, 220hp
Max speed: 35mph
25mph approx cross-country
Range: 110 miles

Designed as an upgunned light tank to replace the M5, the M24 entered service in late 1944. Cadillac and Massey-Harris produced 4,415 vehicles (including variants) by the end of the war. The variants included the M19 GMC, M41 and M37 HMCs, none of which was produced in any quantities before VE-Day. A considerable improvement on the M5, with torsion bar suspension, the M24 was somewhat large for a reconnaissance vehicle.

Howitzer Motor Carriage M7

Crew: 7 (commander, driver, five guncrew)
Length: 19ft 9in
20ft 3.75in (M7B1)
Width: 9ft 5.25in
9ft 7.25in (M7B1)
Height: 8ft 4in
Weight: 50,634lb
50,000lb (M7B1)
Armament: 1×105mm M1A2, M2 or M2A1 howitzer (main)
1×.50cal MG (AA)
Armour: 62mm (max)-12mm (min)

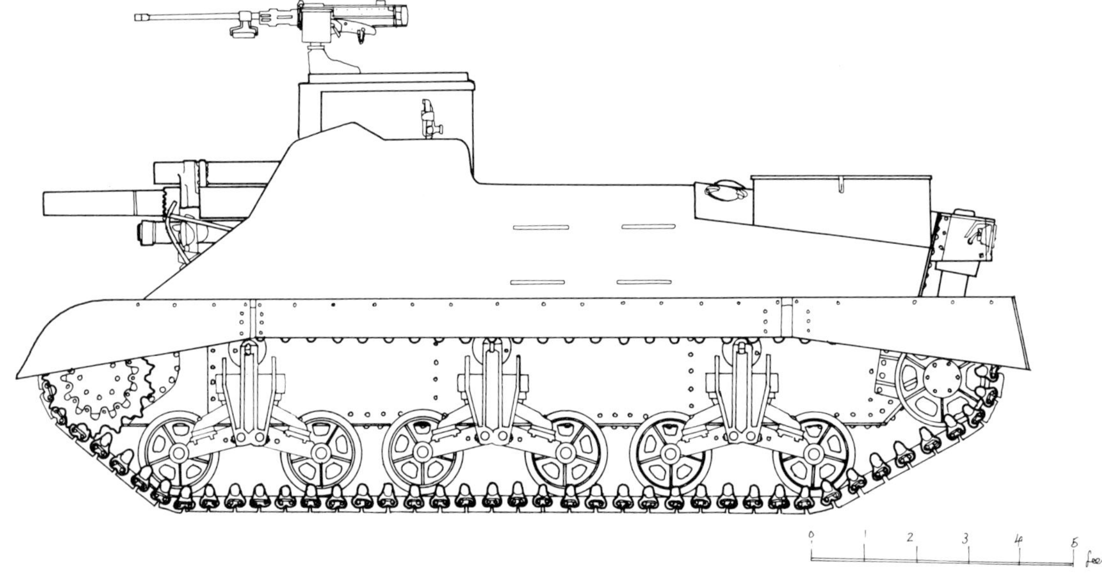

HMC M7 (Priest) showing clearly M3 type bogies, 'pulpit' ring mount for .50cal MG and lack of crew/ammunition protection with shallow side plates; this point was rectified slightly on the M7B1 (based on the M4 chassis) by the inclusion of side plates.

Engine: Continental R-975 radial air-cooled, 350hp
Ford GAA V8, 450hp (M7B1)
Max speed: 25/26mph
20mph (M7B1)
Road range: 85 miles
125 miles (M7B1)

Based on the M3 medium chassis, the first of 2,028 M7s was built by American Loco in 1942. Used by the British and called the Priest, it saw extensive action after El Alamein and was the standard artillery weapon of US armoured divisions. The M7B1, based on the M4A3 chassis, was built in smaller numbers — 806 by Pressed Steel — and differed from the M7 in having hinged side plates for added ammunition/crew protection, a cast one-piece nose and the obvious differences of the M4 chassis — powerplant etc. The 105mm howitzer had a range of 11,160m.

Gun Motor Carriage M12

Crew: 6 (commander, driver, four guncrew)
Length: 22ft 1in
Width: 8ft 9in
Height: 8ft 10in
Weight: 58,000lb
Armament: 1×155mm M1918M1 gun
Engine: Continental R-975 radial petrol, 353hp
Max speed: 24mph
12mph max cross-country
Road range: 140 miles

Using the M1918, a World War 1 weapon of French design, the M12 was the first US SP gun, built on the M3 medium chassis. The

vehicle was equipped with a recoil spade at the rear. 100 were built and, after initial use in the USA for training, a number were overhauled by Baldwin in 1944 for use in Europe after D-Day for heavy bombardment.

Cargo Carrier M30

Crew: 5 (commander, driver, three guncrew)
Length: 19ft 10in
Width: 8ft 9in
Height: 10ft
Weight: 47,000lb
Armament: 1×.50cal MG (AA)
Engine: Continental R-975 radial petrol, 353hp
Max speed: 24mph
12mph max cross-country

Indentical to the M12 without gun and recoil spade, the M30 was used as the latter's limber vehicle, carrying guncrew and ammunition, etc. The M30s were, naturally, produced in equal numbers to the M12s.

Medium Tank M3 Lee/Grant

Crew: 6 (commander, driver, two loaders, two gunners)
Length: 18ft 6in
19ft 8in (M3A4)
Width: 8ft 11in
Height: 10ft 3in
9ft 4in (Grant)
Weight: 60,000lb
Armament: 1×75mm M2/M3 gun (main, sponson-mounted)
1×37mm M5/M6 gun (turret-mounted)
3/4×.30cal Browning MGs

Armour: 37mm (max)-12mm (min)
Engine: Wright radial Continental R-975, 340hp (M3, M3A1)
Twin General Motors 6-71 diesel, 375hp (M3A2, M3A3, M3A5)
Chrysler A-57 Multibank, 370hp (M3A4)
Max speed: 26mph
16mph cross-country
Road range: 120 miles
160 miles (M3A3, M3A5)

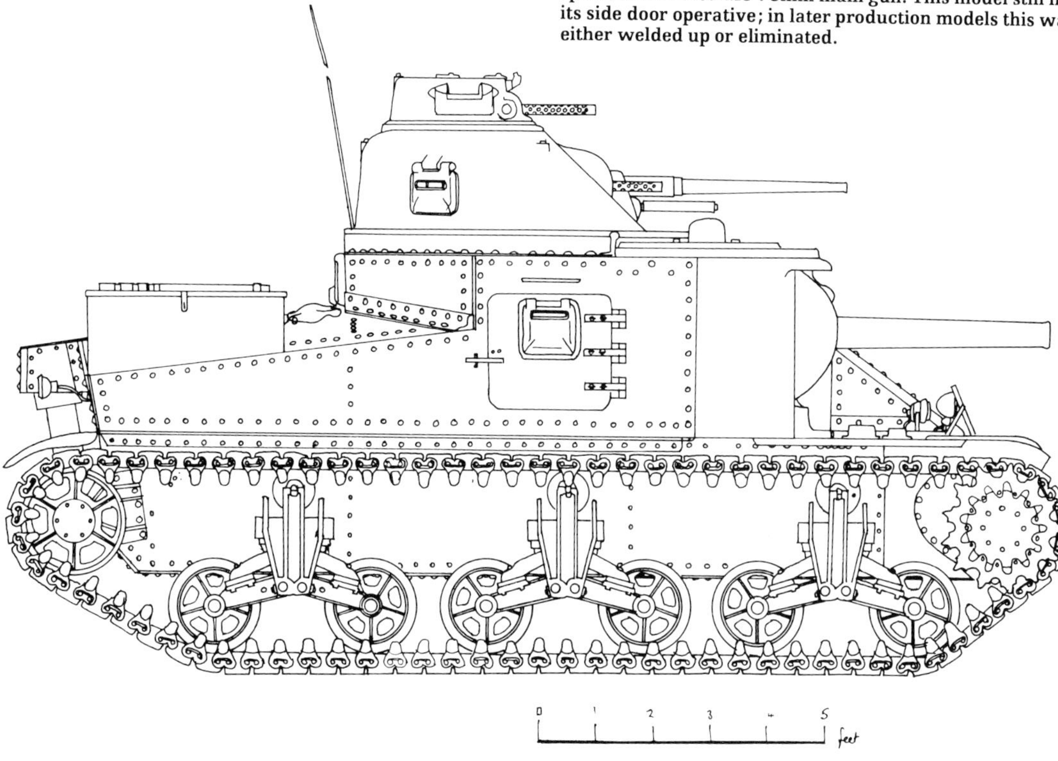

M3A5 (Grant II) showing clearly the riveted hull and sponson-mounted M3 75mm main gun. This model still has its side door operative; in later production models this was either welded up or eliminated.

Evolving from the M2 medium series, the M3 was manufactured at three plants: American Loco, Baldwin Loco and Detroit Arsenal. Over 6,250 were built of all types. There were many variants to the basic hull, including mine exploders, tank recovery vehicles, prime movers and GMCs. It was supplied to the British in two main variants — the Grant without a cupola and the Lee with — and saw action with British forces in the desert and Burma. With its 75mm main gun, it was of considerable help to the British in the western desert; however the drawbacks of a sponson-mounted main gun soon became apparent and it was superseded by the M4 in 1943. By 1944 it had been declared obsolete.

Medium Tank M4 Sherman

Crew: 5 (commander, gunner, loader, driver, co-driver/hull gunner)
Length: 19ft 4in (excluding gun)
Width: 8ft 7in
Height: 9ft
Weight: 66,500lb (M4A1)
69,000lb (M4A2)
68,500lb (M4A3)

M4A4 (Sherman V), the fourth type in production which was built at Detroit Arsenal 1942-43. All M4A4s had a three-piece bolted nose and this type was the one of which most were received by Britain under the Lend-Lease agreements. Note M4 bogies with trailing return rollers as compared to the M3's in the last drawing with the return roller on top of the bracket.

Armament: 1×75mm M3 gun (main)
2×.30cal MGs (secondary, hull and coax)
1×.50cal MG (AA)
Armour: 75mm (max)-12mm (min)
Engine: Continental R-975 air-cooled radial, 420hp (M4A1)
Twin General Motors 6-71 diesels, 375hp (M4A2)
Ford GAA V-8 petrol, 500hp (M4A3)
Chrysler WC Multibank, 370hp (M4A4)
Max speed: 24-29mph
15-20mph cross-country
Road range: 100-150 miles depending on engine

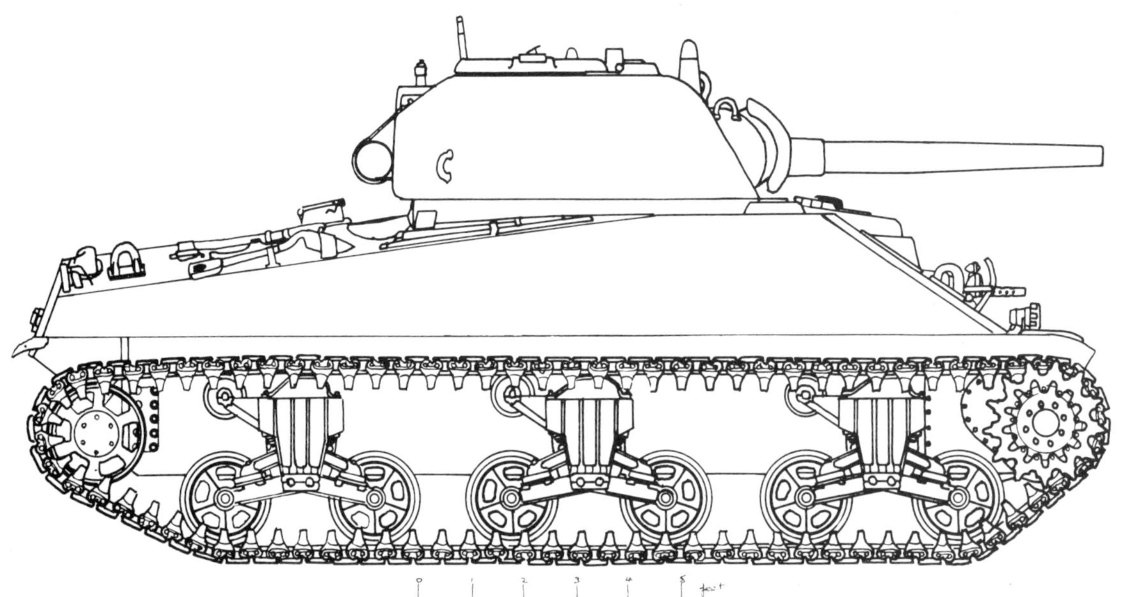

M4 Sherman with 75mm

Crew: 5 (as above)
Length: 24ft 3in
Width: 8ft 9.5in
Height: 9ft 9in

Weight: 70,000-72,800lb
Armament: 1×76mm M1, M1A1, M1A1C or M1A2 gun (main)
1×.50cal MG (AA)

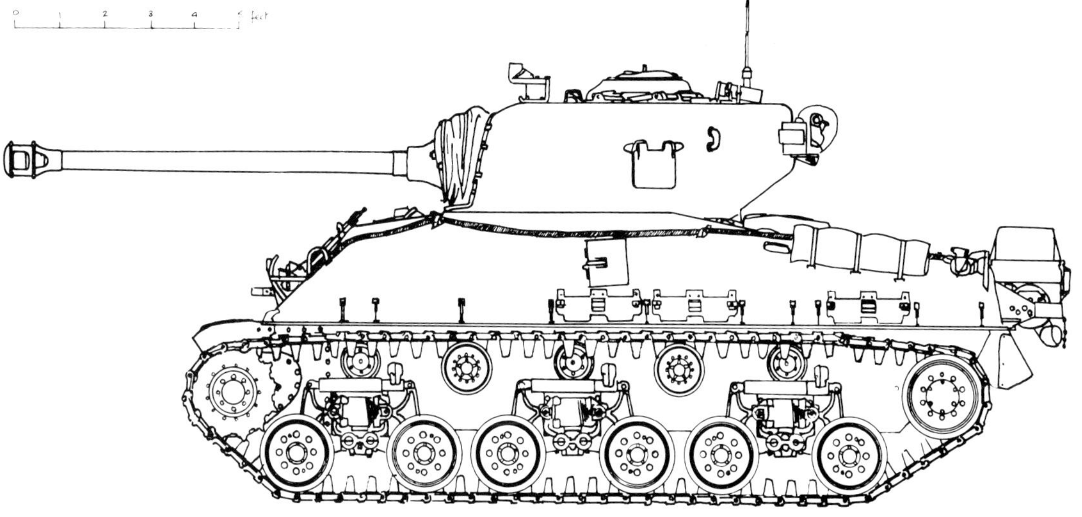

Armour: 62mm (max)-12mm (min)
Engine: Dependent on type
Max speed: 24-29mph
15-20mph cross-country
Road range: 85-100 miles

Over 40,000 M4 series vehicles were built 1942-46, being used by every Allied nation in every theatre of war. Of the basic types, 6,748 M4s were built at Pressed Steel, Baldwin, American Loco, Pullman and Detroit Arsenal plants between July 1942 and January 1944; 6,281 M4A1s were built by Lima, Pressed Steel, Pacific Car & Foundry between February 1942 and November 1943; 8,053 M4A2s were built at Fisher/Grand Blanc, Pullman, American Loco, Baldwin, Federal Welder between April 1942 and December 1943; 3,071 M4A3s were built by Ford and Grand Blanc between June 1942 and March 1945; 7,499 M4A4s were built by Detroit Arsenal July 1942-September 1943; 75 M4A6s were built by Detroit Arsenal October 1943-February 1944.

Most M4s underwent considerable changes during their lifetimes and constant

M4A1 (76mm) with HVSS and M1A1C 76mm main gun. The HVSS — horizontal volute spring suspension — came into being to give a smoother ride for the M4s made heavier by the bigger 76mm gun and internal improvements. With wider tracks, four wheels to each bogie and return rollers on hull sides, HVSS allowed any wheel to be replaced without having to replace the entire bogie.

improvements led to changes within the basic types. The most common change was to the armour, whose early penetration by German tank shells earned the M4 the nickname of 'Ronson Lighter' — because it caught fire every time! This reworking and uparmouring took the form of applique armour, especially on hull sides to protect ammunition stowage, driver and co-driver's hatches and turret sides. Variants included the upgunned M4s with 76mm guns and 105mm howitzers, TRVs, dozers, mine clearing devices, flame throwers, rocket launchers, etc. In British service the M4 also underwent an upgunning, the 75mm being replaced by the 17pdr main gun. When this happened the .30cal hull MG and gunner were dispensed with to increase ammunition stowage and the resulting vehicle was called the Sherman Firefly.

Recovery Vehicle M32

Crew: 5
Length: 19ft 1.25in
Width: 8ft 7in
Height: 9ft
Weight: 62,000lb (loaded)
Armament: 1×81mm mortar
1×.30cal MG (hull)
1×.50cal MG (AA)

Engine: Continental R-975-C1, 350hp
Max speed: 26mph
Road range: 100 miles

A modified M4, this tank recovery vehicle was fitted with an 81mm mortar to fire smoke, a 60,000lb winch and a pivoting A-frame jib.

Heavy Tank M26 Pershing

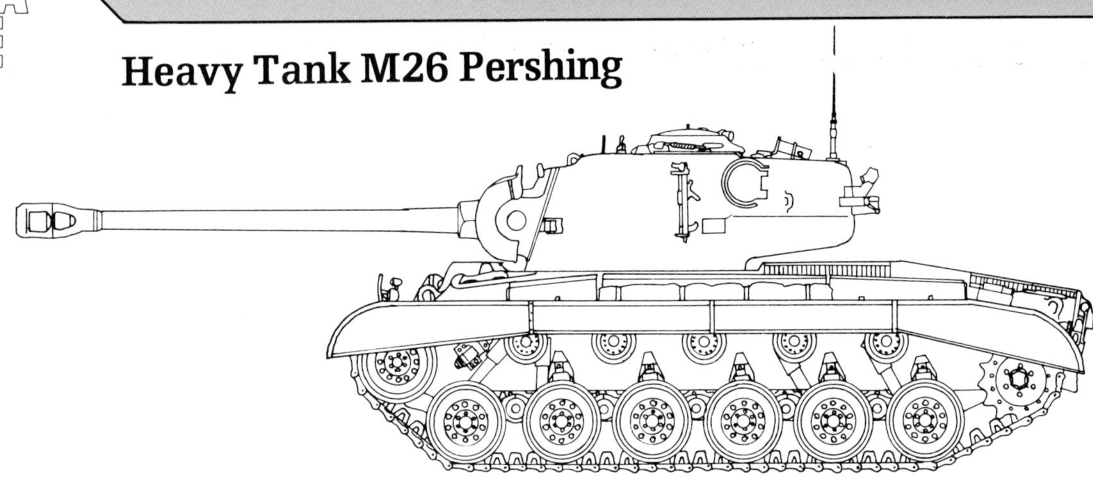

Crew: 5 (commander, driver, co-driver,
gunner, loader)
Length: 28ft 10in
Width: 11ft 6in
Height: 9ft 1in
Weight: 92,000lb
Armament: 1×90mm M3 gun (main)
2×.30cal MGs (secondary, hull and coax)
1×.50cal MG (AA)
Armour: 102mm (max)-13mm (min)
Max speed: 20mph
5.2mph max cross-country
Road range: 92 miles

M26 Pershing with M3 90mm main gun, torsion bar
suspension and vision cupola for commander. The M26
was the first production heavy tank used by the American
Army and which despite a long drawn out testing period,
finally arrived in NW Europe late in 1945 where it proved
itself almost a match for the German Tigers in shoot outs.
The M26 was really one of the new generation of armoured
fighting vehicles and the current US main battle tank, M60,
can trace its ancestry back to this vehicle.

The first 20 T26E3s (later to be standardised as
the M26) were shipped to Europe in January
1945, going to 3rd and 9th Armored Divisions.
Full production began in January 1945 and
Grand Blanc Arsenal built 1,190 between
November 1944 and June 1945, and Detroit

Arsenal manufactured 246, March-June 1945.
Desperately short of heavy tanks, the American
armoured forces clamoured for a vehicle that
could take on the German Panthers and Tigers
after the Battle of the Bulge. The Pershing was
the answer and could well have been seen in
Europe earlier than 1945 had there not been a
decision to keep the M4 production lines
working. As it was the M26 saw limited service
in both Europe and the Pacific.

Gun Motor Carriage M10

Crew: 5 (commander, driver, three guncrew)
Length: 19ft 7in
Width: 10ft
Height: 8ft 1.5in
Weight: 66,000lb
64,000lb (M10A1)
Armament: 1×3in M7 gun (main)
(1×17pdr OQF in Achilles)
1×.50cal Browning MG (AA)
Armour: 50mm (max)-12mm (min)
Engine: Twin GMS 6-71 diesels, 375hp (M10)
Ford GAA V8 petrol, 450hp (M10A1)
Max speed: 30mph
20mph cross-country
Road range: 200 miles

Based on the standard M4 chassis and engines,
the M10 had very different armour (well-
defended front and thinner elsewhere) and an
open turret with a distinctive counterweight on
the rear. It was typical of the US idea of
producing fast, less-armoured vehicles for
battlefield mobility. 4,993 M10s were built at
Grand Blanc Arsenal between October 1942
and September 1943. The M10A1 was the M10
based on the M4A3 chassis and 675 were built
September-November 1943, but most were
kept in the USA or converted into M35 prime
movers or given new turrets and completed as
M36s.

In British service the M10 was known as the

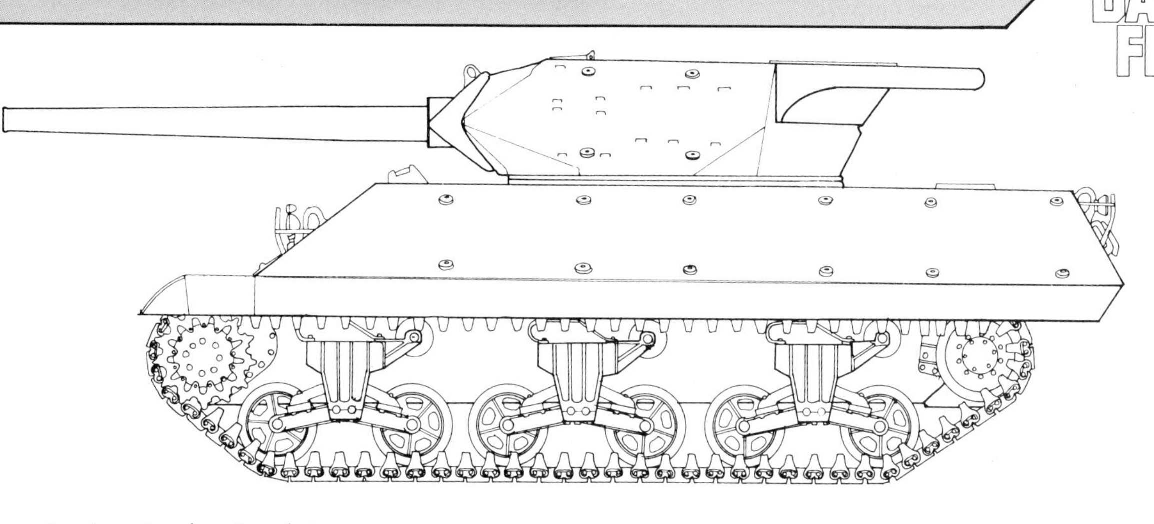

Wolverine and from late 1944 these were converted into Achilles Mk ICs by replacement of the 3in gun with a 17pdr. M10A1s similarly converted were designated Achilles Mk IIC. The Achilles was used extensively postwar.

GMC M10 (Wolverine) showing clearly the counterweight on the turret rear; this was needed to counterbalance the weight of the M7 3in gun.

Gun Motor Carriage M36

Crew: 5 (commander, driver, three guncrew)
Length: 19ft 7in (M36)
20ft 7in (M36B1)
Width: 10ft
Height: 10ft 5.5in (M36)
8ft 9in (M36B1)
Weight: 62,000lb
Armament: 1×90mm M3 gun (main)
1×.50cal MG (AA)
Armour: 50mm (max)-12mm (min)
Engine: Twin GM 6-71 diesels, 375hp (M36B2)
Ford GAA V8 petrol, 450hp (M36, M36B1)
Max speed: 26.25mph
18mph approx cross-country
Road range: 112 miles

Originally tested as an M10 with a 90mm high velocity AA gun, the vehicle was standardised as the M36 and it entered service in late 1944 with very good results against the best German tanks of the period — Panther, Tiger, etc. The M36 was based on the M10A1 chassis and 300 were produced merely by putting a new turret on. 413 were produced in a similar way at American Loco Co, 500 by Massey Harris and 85 by Montreal Loco Co. The M36B1 was an M4A3 fitted with an open topped M36 type turret; Grand Blanc Arsenal produced 187 between October and December 1944. The M36B2 used the M10 hull and 237 were converted from existing M10s by American Loco between April and May 1945.

Gun Motor Carriage M18 Hellcat

Crew: 5 (commander, driver, three guncrew)
Length: 21ft 10in (with gun)
17ft 4in (without)
Width: 9ft 9in
Height: 8ft 5in
Weight: 40,000lb
35,000lb (empty)

Armament: 1×76mm M1A1, M1A1C or M1A2 gun (main)
1×.50cal Browning MG (AA)
Armour: 25mm (max)-7mm (min)
Engine: Continental R-975 air-cooled petrol, 400hp
Max speed: 45-50mph
20mph approx max cross-country

2,507 M18s were built between February and October 1944 by Buick Motor Division of General Motors. Coming under the designation 'Tank Destroyer', the Hellcat was a fast, open turreted armoured vehicle that relied on speed rather than armour to get itself out of trouble.

Halftrack Personnel Carrier M2/M3 and Multiple Gun Motor Carriage M16

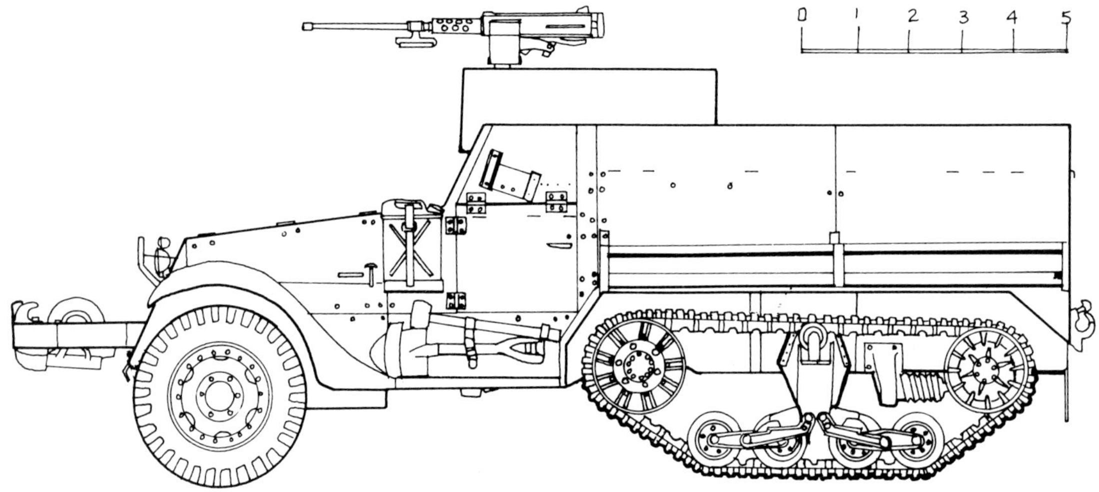

M3A1 showing clearly the 'pulpit' for the M49 ring-mounted .50cal MG. This vehicle is equipped with a winch on the front, others had an unditching roller.

Halftrack Personnel Carrier M2/3

Crew: 3 (commander, driver, co-driver) with seating for 10 in rear
Length: 20ft 2.625in
20ft 6.5in (M3)
Width: 7ft 2.5in (M2)
7ft 3.5in (M3)
Height: 7ft 5in (M2)
8ft 2.5in (M3)
Weight: 19,800lb (M2, loaded)
15,300lb (M2, empty)
20,000lb (M3, loaded)
15,500lb (M3, empty)
Armament: 1×.50cal MG
1×.30cal MG
Armour: 13mm (max)-7mm (min)
Engine: White 160 AX, 147hp
Max speed: 45mph
Road range: 180-215 miles

Multiple Gun Motor Carriage M16

Crew: 5
Length: 21ft 4in
Width: 7ft 1in
Height: 8ft 7in
Weight: 21,600lb (loaded)
18,600lb (empty)
Armament: 4×.50cal MGs
Armour: 13mm (max)-7mm (min)
Engine: White, 142hp
Max speed: 40mph
Road range: 150 miles

The M2 and M3 were the basic personnel carriers of the US Army during World War 2. The M2 was a gun tower with seating for the guncrew and the M3 carried an infantry squad. The M2 had a track running round the inside edge of the superstructure for the MGs, while the M3 had a pedestal mount. 11,415 M2s were built by Autocar (2,992) and White (8,423). 12,499 M3s were built. After 1943 the gun mounts were altered on both vehicles to a ring-mounted 'pulpit' just behind the cab; pintles were also provided for additional MGs. With these new features the vehicles were redesignated M2A1 and M3A1 respectively. From October 1943 they replaced the old M2s and M3s in production and 1,643 M2A1s and

2,862 M3A1s had been built by 1944, when production stopped. Total US production of halftracks reached 41,169 units with variants, which included mortar carriers, gun motor carriages, multiple gun motor carriages and howitzer motor carriages. For example, the multiple gun motor carriage M16: Based on the M3 halftrack, the M16 mounted four .50s in the M45 Maxson turret. 724 were built by White in 1942-43.

Dimensions for the whole M2/M3 family depend on whether a winch or roller is fitted on the front, whether a .50cal is fitted and whether there are racks on the sides.

Armoured Car M8 Greyhound and Armoured Utility Car M20

Crew: 4 (driver, co-driver, gunner, commander)
2-6 (M20)
Length: 16ft 5in
Width: 8ft 4in
Height: 7ft 4.5in
7ft 7in (M20)
Weight: 17,400lb (loaded)
17,500lb (M20 loaded)
Armament: 1×37mm M6 gun (main)
1×.30cal MG (secondary, coax)
1×.50cal MG (AA) (only armament in M20)
Armour: 20mm (max)-3mm (min)
Engines: Hercules JXD petrol, 110hp
Max speed: 56mph
Road range: 350 miles

Adopted from the T22 project, the M8 Greyhound, as it was called by the British, was

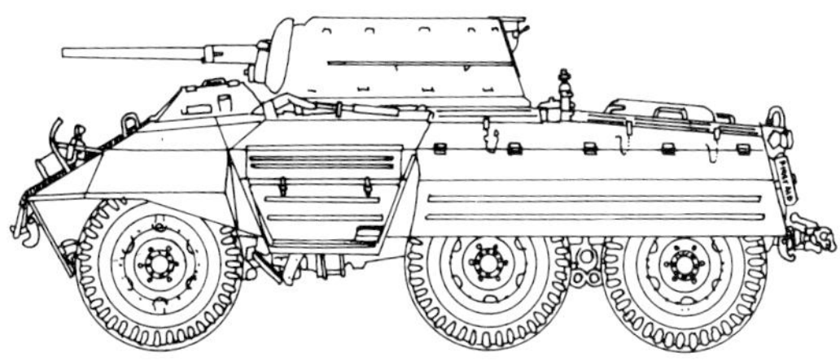
M8 Greyhound armoured car.

the main armoured car of the US Army during World War 2. 8,523 were built by Ford Motor Company by the end of the war. Very fast and very quiet, its chassis was used for the M20 utility car, of which 3,791 were built by Ford; data for the latter is similar to the M8 without turret and 37mm gun, which were replaced by a superstructure mounting a .50cal machine gun on a ring mount.

Armoured Car T17E1 Staghound

Crew: 5 (driver, co-driver, gunner, loader, commander)
Length: 18ft
Width: 8ft 10in
Height: 7ft 9in
Weight: 30,700lb
Armament: 1×37mm (main)
2×.30cal MGs (secondary, hull and coax)
1×.30cal MG (AA)
Armour: 45mm (max)-7mm (min)
Engine: Two GMC 270, 97hp
Max speed: 56mph
Road range: 450 miles

Built for the British Army by the Chevrolet Company, between 1942 and 1943 2,844 were manufactured. In British service it was called the Staghound I, the Staghound II having a 76.2mm howitzer and the Staghound III a

T17E1 Staghound built by the Chevrolet Company for the British Army between 1942 and 1943. Armed with a 37mm gun.

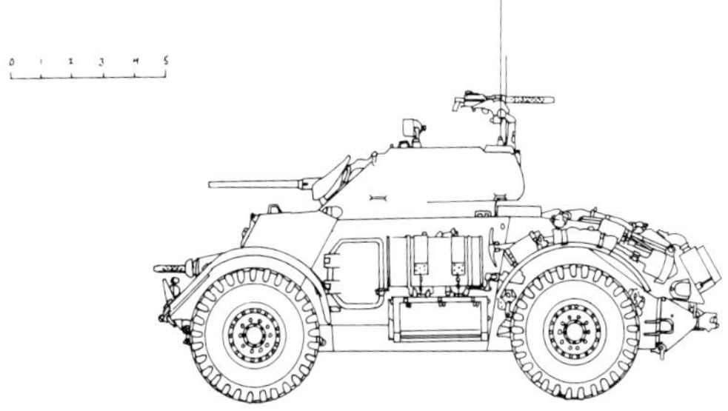

Crusader tank turret. A Staghound AA vehicle (designated T17E2 by the Americans) was also produced with a Frazer Nash turret. Many of these had their turrets removed and were used as command cars.

Above: **Heavily camouflaged M4 in the ruins of Bijude, Belgium. This British vehicle has a .30cal M1919A4 AA machine gun and its 'pistol port' (in British parlance) is open. This hatch served the dual purpose of venting fumes from the turret and enabling spent cartridge cases to be ejected.**

Top right: **How many men can you get on a tank? — 2 Heavily sandbagged M4s (the one in the foreground armed with a 76mm main gun) roll in to Heppenheim, Germany, 27 March 1945, under a fluttering white flag of surrender.**

Right: **British M4 Sherman having just crossed a Bailey bridge: note mound of equipment on rear decking, including the ubiquitous ration box, and jerricans — a German one on the right and a British model on the left.**

ANN SCHAFER

Right: **M4 with considerable applique armour to hull sides and front, and turret sides outside Cherbourg in 1944. Just above the M34A1 gun mount is one of the tankers' distinctive crash helmets; also lying on the hull front is an M3 SMG.**

Right inset: **M4 of US Ninth Army advancing (!?) through muddy conditions. Note tankers' helmets and windcheaters, stowage on front hull including wire on the left, applique armour on driver's and co-driver's hatches and three-piece bolted nose. The censor has obliterated most of the markings on the hull front, although the triangular armoured designation is just visible to the left and HQ discernible on the right.**

Above: With the twin spires of Cologne cathedral in the background, infantrymen take cover behind a 76mm-armed M4 which has extended grousers on its tracks, and whose .50cal machine gun is in the stowed position at the back of the turret, its barrel removed.

Right: US Seventh Army vehicles moving through the bombed out streets of Nuremberg, 20 April 1945. German civilians can be seen carrying water behind the tanks, which are an interesting mixture of M4A3s armed with 76mm main guns and (at right) a 75mm-armed M4. The M4A3s have T23 turrets, M1A1C guns and HVSS.

Left: **M4** of the Third Army outside Metz giving a clear indication of vehicle marking under rear deck stowage. The marking indicates this vehicle to be the 10th in Company B, 735th Tank Battalion of XX Corps. Vehicle markings, unlike those of aircraft, were always slightly nebulous and often concealed in the battle area for intelligence reasons. They were divided into four groups of letters which denoted (from left to right): army, corps or division codes; regimental or battalion codes; company codes; and, finally, vehicle numbering codes. The first either gave the army number, with an A after it to signify army, or the corps number (in Roman numerals) or the division; the second, the squadron or battalion code, was followed by a branch or service symbol (in this case a triangle to denote armoured; other well used symbols were TD — Tank Destroyer, AA — Anti-Aircraft, E — Engineer, I — Infantry); the company codes were given in letter form (thus HQ for HQ company); and vehicles were numbered in sequence to show their march order. The 745th Tank Battalion was a unit attached to an armoured division which came under XX Corps' jurisdiction.

Left: **M4s on the road to Avranches during the breakout from Normandy. This photograph shows clearly the .50cal machine gun's carrying handle — after firing the barrel could be removed and the handle kept flesh away from hot metal.**

Above: Concerto in C at **Monde St Etienne, 16 January 1944, showing the effects of 88mm anti-tank shells. The 88mm, renowned both in its anti-aircraft and anti-tank roles, fired a 22lb AP shot with a muzzle velocity of 2,650ft/sec. As a tank gun, it could penetrate most Allied armoured vehicles and armed the Jagdpanther (Pak L/70), Tiger I (KwK36 L/56) and Tiger II (Königstiger, KwK43 L/71).**

Right: **British Shermans during the battle for Caen, 11 July 1944.**

Left: Heavily camouflaged M4 engaging enemy targets across the Marne with both .50cal and 75mm guns. Obviously posed for the photographer, this picture does give a clear indication of the lack of turret overhang on the Sherman when it was traversed to 90 degrees, indicating lack of stowage space, room for which had to be made up in the hull.

Below left: British **M4A4** Shermans during the breakout from Normandy: note stowage box on turret rear.

Right: Canadian **M4A4** advancing during Operation Goodwood.

Below: **M4A1** on the road to Brittany during Operation Goodwood: note the distinctive curve of the M4A1's cast hull.

US 77

CAUTION
LEFT
HAND
DRIVE
NO SIGNALS

Above left: **M4s roll out of an LST at Anzio, Italy. The two vehicles show the different tracks to be found on American armoured vehicles, the M4 in the foreground having the all-steel type, and the one following has the addition of rubber chevrons to reduce wear and noise.**

Left: **Troops of US Third Army moving towards Argentan, 1944, past a British Sherman.**

Above: **Canadian Shermans advancing towards the River Orne south of Caen during the breakout from Normandy. Note the all-steel tracks on this vehicle and the rubber chevroned type on hull nose.**

Right: **M4A1s of a British unit in the bocage country of Normandy.**

Left: There seems to have been a misjudgement here! A heavily camouflaged M4 has taken a nose dive while trying to emulate the infantry in front in fording a canal.

Below left: M4A3 (76mm) with HVSS.

Right: M4A1 (76mm) with 75mm-armed M4s.

Below: Sherman VC Firefly, the designation given by the British to M4A4s rearmed with British 17pdr main gun. Most Firefly conversions were based on the M4A4, which was the main Lend-Lease variant — the US Army using the M4A3 as its prime variant. Note the three-piece bolted nose, which all M4A4s had, lack of bow machine gun to increase ammunition stowage (Fireflies also lost the co-driver), extensive barrel camouflage, distinctive 17pdr gun muzzle and the use of helmets to protect driving lights. The Firefly was the only British vehicle in service in mid-1944 that was a match for the German armoured vehicles and it was, indeed, a better weapon than the 76mm-armed American M4 counterpart.

Left: **M4** with dozer blade crossing a recently laid bridge. The soldiers on guard for the cameraman are carrying M1 rifles and the man in the foreground has a rifle grenade discharger attached to his.

Right: **M4** with dozer attachment bursting out of Aachen station, 1945. The dozer was first attached to Shermans in Italy in 1943 and proved so successful that a special dozer blade, the M1, was made for the M4 itself. Attached to the middle bogie on each side it was powered hydraulically from the tank's power traverse. The triangular armour immediately behind the blade is an armoured cover for the lifting gear.

Below: **M4** on the outskirts of Caen during Operation Goodwood, the breakout from Normandy.

Two views of the British Sherman ARV. *Below left,* alongside a Bedford truck of 11 Armoured Division (note marking on left mudguard). *Left,* rear view showing equipment stowage — planks, tow bars and jerricans. The ARV Mk I had a winch in place of the turret and a collapsible A frame jib; the Mk II had a dummy fixed turret with jibs at back and front, an earth spade and a 25ton winch.

Right: M32 tank recovery vehicle based on the standard M4 chassis with a fixed turret, 60,000lb winch and pivoting A frame jib. This M32, moving at speed through a German town, has tarpaulins covering its A frame at back and a profusion of water/fuel cans on rear decking. On the hull side there are spare sprockets, attached to the turret spare roadwheels and, between the middle frames of the three-piece bolted nose, there is a tow hook.

Below: Vehicles of 2nd Gordons, 15th Division, preparing to advance. At right is a Sherman Crab, one of the many anti-mine devices tried on the M4 chassis. The Crab was a British design based on the earlier Lobster. Developed in 1943, a brigade of 79th Armoured Division was equipped with Sherman Crabs for use during the Normandy landings. The Crab's flail had 43 chains, drive for the rotation coming through a power cut-off from the engine. To the left is a Lloyd carrier.

The T34 Calliope rocket launcher was mounted experimentally on M4s in the latter part of the war. Calliope was made up of 60 4.5in rocket launchers mounted in three groups of 36, 24 and 24. Traverse and elevation were accomplished by movements of turret and gun of the parent vehicle. First used in August 1944, Calliope saw limited service in World War 2. (*Left*) This view shows the elevating bar attached to the M4's 75mm main gun. (*Below*) Section of Calliope-equipped M4s with supply lorries carrying reloads. (*Right*) Reloading the chambers of Calliope. (*Below right*) Calliope-equipped M4 unit ready to fire.

Above: **M26 Pershings of 2nd Armoured Division, Ninth US Army, passing the town hall in Magdeburg, Germany, 18 April 1945. Armed with a 90mm main gun, Pershings saw action in the ETO (European Theatre of Operations) only in the last days of the war, although they saw more action in the Pacific. The M26 was the Americans' first 'heavy' tank of the war, put in to production only after the Ardennes offensive of 1944/45 caused their forces in Europe to complain of the M4's light armour and, even in the 76mm-armed form, under-gunning when compared to German front line AFVs.**

Top right: **Gun Motor Carriage (GMC) M10 firing across the River Loire at Orleans; note stowage in characteristic position on turret sides and the counterweight at turret rear — necessary to compensate for the weight of the M7 3in gun.**

Right: **GMC M10 firing on German border towns, 1945.**

Left and below: Two views of GMC M10s firing their 3in guns on the outskirts of Aachen. Note censor-deleted markings, curve of counterweight and considerable stowage on both vehicles.

Right: GMC M10 on the road to Vossenach, Germany, checking the route on a map which the censor has deleted. Aside from the 3in main gun (far left) and standard .50cal AA machine gun (right foreground) the vehicle has been upgunned with the inclusion of another .50cal machine gun (centre left) and a .30cal machine gun (centre right); note sandbags on open turret front.

Left: A camouflaged M10 moving through Percy directed by an MP, whose Harley Davidson motorcycle is on the left of the photograph. The standard motorcycle of the US Army, it carried a holster for an M1 rifle.

Below left: GMC M10, in service with a British unit, after landing in France. In the background to the left there is a Churchill AVRE armed with a spigot mortar (called a 'Petard' it was of 29cm calibre) and, above the beachhead, barrage balloons.

Top right: GMC M10 on the outskirts of Artena, Italy, with Fifth Army (5A) all that can be made out from the markings.

Centre right: The British called the M10 tank destroyer the Wolverine, when it was equipped with its standard US issue 3in gun. From late 1944 these Wolverines were upgunned by replacement of the main armament with a 17pdr, which made the vehicle a much more efficient tank destroyer known as the Achilles. The 17pdr had a muzzle velocity of 2,900ft/sec and could penetrate 120mm of armour at 500yd. This photograph shows Achilles IICs of Polish 1st Armoured Division on manoeuvres in England, June 1944.

Bottom right: A view of Achilles, again under the Polish flag. This view shows the elliptical marker on the left hand side of the rear of the vehicle which identified its Polish possession (the ellipse has PL inside), and gives an excellent closeup of the M10's counterbalancing turret weight. This vehicle has both .50cal and .30cal machine guns fitted, two spare roadwheels stowed on rear decking and spare track links affixed to the turret side to give added armour protection to the thinner areas there. The M10 was a product of the American 'mobility before protection' doctrine and while its armour was well sloped at the front it had a thickness of only 50mm — compared to the M4's 75mm. It could, however, manage 30mph and had better hitting power than the M4, the M7 3in gun able to penetrate 96.3mm of armour at 1,000yd.

Left: **GMC M36 crossing a temporary bridge over the River Rhine at Worms.**

Bottom left: **GMC M36, an effective and efficient tank destroyer mounting an M3 90mm main gun on an M10A1 hull (which in turn was based on the M4A3 medium tank chassis).**

Below: **GMC M36 during the Ardennes campaign.**

Left: Civilians at Dusseldorf line the streets to watch GMC M18s of US First Army drive through the city. Unofficially known as the Hellcat, the M18 was armed with a 76mm main gun (here in its M1A1C version) and was one of the fastest armoured vehicles of World War 2. It was a popular vehicle for its speed and reliability of suspension which was of the torsion bar type.

Below left: GMC M18 Hellcats showing clearly the clean cut lines of the glacis plate. In the background are two M8 armoured cars.

Right: US Engineers of 94th Infantry Division prepare anti-tank mines in front of an M18 Hellcat. This vehicle has been given a coat of whitewash for snow camouflage — and as most of the snow seems to have melted the effect will be quite the opposite to that intended!

Below: M18 showing compact configuration and turret layout.

Above: Firing the .50cal machine gun from an extended mount on an M3 halftrack, with the dust from the recoil swirling everywhere. This M3 has a considerable load of equipment which includes a number of stretchers.

Left: M3A1 showing clearly the rear door by which the infantry carrying M3 or M3A1 differed from the M2 and M2A1. This vehicle has the characteristic baggage stowage of the M3, two .30cal machine guns mounted on pintles on the sides of the rear compartment, and a ring-mounted .50cal machine gun.

Above: **M3 halftrack belonging to 46th Armored Infantry Battalion of 5th Armored Division (note marking on front bumper). This vehicle has a winch on the front (all M2/M3s had either this or an unditching roller) and a .50cal machine gun on a pedestal mount.**

Above right: **One of the most frequent, and successful, adaptations of the halftrack chassis to GMC use was the addition of a 75mm gun. This vehicle, a prototype with an M3 main gun instead of the usual M1897A, was designated T73. Note unditching roller at front.**

Right: **M2A1 following an M5 light tank towards St Lo. Just visible below the .50cal machine gun is the M49 ring mount, which was the main difference between the M2 and the M2A1. The M2 was designed as a carrying vehicle for an artillery gun crew.**

Baldy

Left: The crew of a US Ninth Army M16 keep a good watch out for aircraft. The jeep behind has an AA board on its radiator grille indicating its service and has had its mudguards extended to the front in what was a fairly common field modification.

Below: A view of the Maxson M45 turret on M16 *Baldy*. Note gunner's position inside turret, cartridge feed mechanism and extra magazine stowage. On the left front of the vehicle there is a Thompson .45cal sub-machine gun in a holster fitting.

Top left: **Multiple Gun Motor Carriage M16 on AA defence near the Ludendorff Bridge at Remagen, as US First Army troops cross the Rhine. The M16 mounted four .50cal machine guns in a Maxson M45 turret. The vehicle is surrounded by a litter of cartridge cases, empty magazines and the lookout lazing at the rear is noticeably close to his binoculars. Note cutout in folded side flap to allow turret rotation when the sides were up.**

Left: **Another multiple gun motor carriage based on the M3 halftrack was the M15/15A1. It combined two .50cal machine guns with a 37mm cannon; the M15's .50s were mounted above the 37mm, the M15A1's below. This photograph shows an M15A1's 37mm gun being loaded with nine-round clips of ammunition.**

Above: **With the French Tricolour flying on the Arc de Triomphe for the first time in four years, an M8 armoured car takes part in the Liberation of Paris parade. Note commander's radio microphone, ring mount for .50cal machine gun and good view of the coax machine gun, main 37mm gun and sighting telescope on turret front.**

Top: **M8 armoured cars in St Sever Calvados, Brittany, during Third Army's breakout from Normandy. Nicknamed the Greyhound, the M8 had a 37mm main gun and .50cal AA machine gun as armament, the latter mounted here on a ring mount.**

Above: **M8 armoured car, here with its .50cal machine gun on a pintle mount: note chains on wheels for improved traction in heavy going, aerials tied back and lack of side skirts.**

Right: **M8s heading towards Cologne past the bombed out remains of a brewery. The lead vehicle is towing a standard ¼ton trailer while the second has one of more dubious origins. Presumably some of the considerable amount of equipment stowed has been similarly liberated!**

Left: The M8 was the progenitor of the M20 utility car, with a superstructure replacing the 37mm gun turret and an armament of only a ring-mounted .50cal machine gun. This M20 of a US Seventh Army Cavalry Recce Squadron is having its equipment stowage checked next to one of the Maginot Line pillboxes. Note absence of side skirts and chains on wheels.

Below: Victory parade through Paris — M20 utility cars following a tank recovery vehicle and a jeep.

Right: General Verney, GOC 7th Armored Division, entering Ghent on 8 September 1944, in his Staghound.

Below right: T17E1 Staghound Mk I *The Baron*. Built to British specifications and used specifically by them, the Staghound was armed with a 37mm main gun, .30cal coax and bow machine guns. This vehicle lacks its side fuel drum, the brackets for which can be seen between the wheels.

BASS
BELL
MOR HE

THE
BARON
F214233
47

Above: **Staghound of British Eighth Army entering S Arzilla, Italy, during attacks on the Gothic Line, September 1944.**

Below: **British Staghound armoured cars.**